NATIONAL PARKS
OF THE
AMERICAN WEST

NATIONAL PARKS OF THE AMERICAN WEST

Photography by Karyn Chauve & J.F. Regnier

WELLFLEET

We would like to thank the National Park Service, especially the National Park Rangers
whose kindness and assistance helped make this book possible
and Frank, Tony and Carmela for everything.

To our parents
Suzanne and Lionel Chauve
Marie Louise and Paul Regnier

All photography courtesy of Karyn Chauve & J.F. Regnier except for the following:
Courtesy of Badlands National Park, *284-286*
Courtesy of Mount Rushmore National Memorial, *280-282, 286*
Courtesy of Petrified Forest Museum Association, *174-178*
Courtesy of Jim Peaco, Yellowstone National Park, *215, 222, 240-244*

Publishing Director: Frank Oppel
Editorial Director: Tony Meisel
Design Director: Carmela Pereira
Editor: Theresa Stiles
Composition: Meadowcomp Ltd.
Origination by Regent Publishing Services Limited
Printed by Leefung-Asco Printers Limited

Manufactured in Hong Kong
ISBN: 1-55521-671-4

CONTENTS

Introduction   7

Arches National Park   9

Big Bend National Park   19

Bryce Canyon National Park   31

Canyonlands National Park   41

Capitol Reef National Park   51

Carlsbad Caverns National Park   59

Crater Lake National Park   63

Waterton/Glacier International Peace Park   71

Grand Canyon National Park   83

Grand Teton National Park   95

Great Basin National Park   107

Guadalupe Mountains National Park   117

Lassen Volcanic National Park   127

Mesa Verde National Park   133

Mount Rainier National Park   145

North Cascades National Park   155

Olympic National Park   161

Petrified Forest National Park   173

Redwood National Park   179

Rocky Mountain National Park   187

Sequoia/Kings Canyon National Parks   205

Yellowstone National Park   213

Yosemite National Park   245

Zion National Park   257

National Monuments and Recreation Areas   265

Mount Rushmore National Memorial   279

Badlands National Park   283

Index   287

INTRODUCTION

'The Best Idea America Ever Had'

PERHAPS ONLY a new country, one that made a virtue of casting aside the strictures of its old European heritage—and a country filled with natural wonders and blessed with abundant room, at that—could afford the idea of preserving vast tracts of land simply for its citizens to enjoy. Not to graze animals upon, or to cut over or mine, or even to live on—there was plenty of room for that; no, just to visit, to see, to *enjoy*. Certainly the Old World was filling up with memorials and museums, and even manicured city parks, but these were to preserve or show off the works of man. Raw land, beautiful though it may be, was to be put into harness. From where came this revolutionary idea of saving it untouched?

Contrary to present perception, 19th-century America was not populated entirely with tycoons, trappers, boosters, Babbits and empire-builders; there were many thoughtful Americans who looked back—or at least around—as well as strictly forward. They saw that animal species were dying away, that historic artifacts from Colonial times were disappearing and that age-old natural splendors were being pillaged for short-term profit. The idea of preserving land by decree was first made public in 1832, when George Catlin, the artist who became famous for his paintings of American Indian cultures, wrote down his wish that they might be safeguarded by "some great protecting policy of the government . . . in a magnificent park . . . . A nation's park, containing man and beast, in all wildness and freshness of their nature's beauty." It is an indication of how unpopulated all of America was then if he was able to suggest the entire country west of the Mississippi River be so exempted.

And it happened—although on a vastly smaller scale and not exactly to the benefit of Catlin's beloved Native Americans. In that same year, 1832, the federal government took the first step toward such a policy by setting aside a reservation in Arkansas, which is now Hot Springs National Park. Progress came slowly but accelerated all the way. In 1864, Congress took time away from the Civil War to give the Yosemite Valley to the state of California to be "held for public use, resort, and recreation." (Afterward it took the valley, and more land around it, back and placed it within the National Park Service.) A decade later, in 1872, came the watershed. Congress put Yellowstone aside as a public, national park—the first of its kind in the world. (In fact, legislators had to be convinced first that the land was worthless for agriculture, but preservationists didn't mind.) The Department of the Interior was charged with administering the new holding, but without experience in such duties, or even a staff to carry them out, the

Interior Secretary asked the Secretary of War for Army engineer and then cavalry units to run the new entity. In those times "rangering" at Fort Yellowstone was more than steering tourists away from the chipmunks; several times in the park's first decade, hostile Indians chased visitors and soldiers out of Yellowstone, and in following years prospectors, trappers and loggers were chased out too—this time by the soldiers.

In the 1890s, four more national parks were created—by an act of Congress, as they must be—all in the West: Sequoia, Mount Rainier, Yosemite and General Grant (which became Kings Canyon). Then, in 1906, under pressure from voters concerned about the pillaging of Indian ruins on the Colorado Plateau, Congress passed the Antiquities Act. This gave the president the power to save public lands with "features of historic and scientific interest" from imminent despoliation by proclaiming them national monuments. Later on, when the immediate danger was gone and Congress could weigh the action, many monuments became parks. The first site to become a national monument was Devils Tower, in Wyoming, which was so named by President Theodore Roosevelt.

While these wilderness areas of the West were being collected, the attention of preservationists also turned to the settled East. There the war department had been lobbying successfully to preserve, on its own, a number of Revolutionary and Civil War battlefields as historic sites. By 1916, the United States had 35 national parks and monuments, and a management problem. The National Park Service was formed in that year, under the Organic Act, within the Department of the Interior, with a formal charge to conserve these areas' "scenery and the natural and historic objects and the wild life therein and to provide for the enjoyment of the same in such manner and by such means as will leave them unimpaired for the enjoyment of future generations." The new service formed a corps of uniformed rangers to do just that.

Within 20 years, all federal preserves (which do not include national forests and national wildlife refuges; they are managed by the Forest Service and the Fish and Wildlife Service, and the former are often open to logging, mining and other commercial uses) had been taken from other branches of the government and placed under the jurisdiction of the Park Service. America had a unified, national system of public parks.

AMERICA's national lands today encompass more than 80 million acres administered by the National Park Service in the public trust. No other nation on earth has left its children such a rich and varied legacy. Another 100 million acres could—and probably should—be preserved in this manner.

As the 20th century draws to a close, 47 states of the Union—as well as Guam, the Virgin Islands, Puerto Rico and the District of Columbia—contain more than 320 national parks, monuments, recreation areas, sea- and lakeshores, military parks, historical parks, battlefields, cemeteries, memorials, parkways, preserves, historic sites, riverways and scenic trails. In scope and locale, they range from the Gates of the Arctic, in northern Alaska, to Ellis Island, in New York Harbor, and from Florida's Biscayne Park to the War in the Pacific Park in Guam. This book is a photographic journey through parks of the West, from the Olympic Peninsula and Glacier Park on the Canadian border, south to Big Bend, on the Texas side of the Rio Grande. More and more groan under the accumulated weight of their visitors; a few still seem almost as wild and as the day they became wards of the government.

Though their enabling legislations invariably speak of "eternal preservation" what man has set aside, man can reopen, or merely change. Controversies have flourished in and around the national parks. Should a railroad be built through Yellowstone? That question came before Congress in 1886, and many legislators felt it was "absurd" to place the interests of animals ahead of the "demands of commerce." The railroad lost, however. Hetch Hetchy, in Yosemite Park, and Glen Canyon, on the Colorado River above the Grand Canyon, were less fortunate; both drowned by vast dams. Today, as America's environmental conscience comes to full flower in the 1990s, the national parks and monuments were never safer. But the price of their safety is eternal vigilance.

ARCHES
NATIONAL PARK
Utah

A Natural Stonehenge

EYE OF THE WHALE. Marching Men. Dark Angel. The Tower of Babel. Three Gossips. Parade of Elephants . . . .

There are dozens more, with equally graphic names—and hundreds more, which have never been named and are hardly ever seen by visitors who stick to the trails, that also belong to this fabulous collection of geologic oddities. They are the natural sandstone arches, hoodoos, buttes, rock windows (arches-to-be; anything with an opening less than 3 feet across is called a window), pinnacles and sculpted figures and monoliths of Arches National Park. In this small area of the red-rock country of southeastern Utah lies the largest collection of these rock arches in the world; more than 200 have been discovered to date, and there may still be a few not yet known. Generations from now there will likely be a few less, yet in another millennium there may be a few more. For all these structures are constantly changing, but usually very slowly: forming, wearing down and dying; responding to wind, earth tremors, tectonic shifting and the destructive freeze-and-thaw cycles of the weather.

The changes don't always come at a geologic pace, however. An arch suspended seemingly for eternity across the blue desert sky may, from one moment to the next, come crashing down. A critical chunk, a keystone, gives way after eons of shouldering tremendous loads of compression or tension. It drops to the ground suddenly, perhaps spalling off from the center span of its arch as a few drops of rain water in a crack behind it freeze and expand—and the rest of the formation crashes to earth along with it. A rare occurrence, to be sure, but an inevitability nonetheless. Arch-building can take place as quickly too: Sometime in the 1940s, Skyline Arch, at the campground near Devil's Garden, in the northern end of the park, suddenly doubled in size.

Barring an earthquake, the forces that shape and eventually destroy these stone arches are the same nagging little quirks of nature that peel paint off our houses and buckle the pavement in our driveways. But arches are born in regional upheavals, slow-motion cataclysms that would ignore the paint and turn our houses and driveways upside-down en masse.

Arches National Park's 73,000 acres sit atop a so-called salt dome, a thick underground bed of salt that was left behind when a prehistoric ocean evaporated away, some 200 million to 300 million years ago. Then, for millions of years afterward, gravels, sands, clays and dust were laid down over the salt by wind, running water and even other seas or lakes. These layers, under ever greater pressure as the thickness built up overhead—perhaps to as much as a mile in all—were slowly compressed into rock, an enormous regional formation now called the Entrada Sandstone. But the salt beneath was not. Such depositions are notoriously unstable; salt can't compress into rock. In fact, under pressure it begins to move—to shift, and even liquify and flow to zones where the burden is momentarily less. This warping of the basement spells disaster for the crust of rock above.

Huge cracks, or faults, opened up in the earth of what would be Arches Park. Whole blocks of stone were thrust upward; sections broke off like slow-motion calving icebergs and toppled sideways. Other pieces slumped downwards between the gashes in the rocks. Along the Moab Fault, which can be seen from the Visitor Center at the entrance to the park, beds of once-adjacent rock were moved almost half a mile apart.

In many places, long, roughly parallel cracks in the sandstone opened up, resembling corrugations in a sheet of cardboard. Then, once the blank face of the rock was fissured, wind and water got in and went to work, expanding the cracks. As more and more surface area became exposed, the process speeded up. Precipitation got into the porous sandstone, freezing and expanding, thawing and contracting, dissolving certain minerals, flowing always farther in and down. Wind cleared the new rock dust away, exposing more stone to the weather. Eventually, over millions of years, the cracks became ravines, bigger than the blocks they separated, and the blocks wore down to what geologists call fins. This set the stage for arch formation. Differential erosion attacked softer or weaker sections of the fins, zones where the original sediment had perhaps been poorly sorted, leaving a mixture of grain sizes that couldn't compact together.

Suddenly, in fin after fin, core material gave way and crumbled to the ground. Usually the entire structure followed. But in some cases, fins with the proper delicate balance of hardness, shape, size and other physical properties could stand alone, without their missing middles. The windows became larger with the passing of more time, as weather continued to quarry out the remaining rock. The result, the end product of unimaginable spans of time, was another span—a stone bridge that seems to reach from the past to the present day.

Landscape Arch, at 300 feet, is the longest in the park, standing 90 feet from the ground at its apex and narrowing to 6 feet thick. Despite the tons of stone within it, the arch has an airy, delicate feel about it, much like the best suspension bridges made by man. Natural wonders is exactly what these formations are, but some early explorers reported they'd found the ruined structures of a lost civilization.

MAN'S PRESENCE is hardly felt at Arches. Park Service facilities are minimal; no food or lodging is available. The desert climate keeps visitors in or not too far from their cars. And there are only three roads in the park suitable for ordinary passenger cars. The sleepy town of Moab, Utah, lies five miles from the south entrance (the only entrance) on the other side of the Colorado River, but it seems to have little effect on the park. Like all of the great southwestern desert, Arches is a place of eternal silences and sweeping vistas, freezing nights and furnace-like days, flash floods and bone-dry dust, still blue skies, violent purple storms and glowing red sunsets. But unlike much of the desert, which has been opened up to visitors by aircraft, riverboats and four-wheel-drives, Arches still seems to sleep relatively undisturbed.

A few mule deer feed among the stunted piñon pines and junipers. Foxes and golden eagles hunt kangaroo rats, jackrabbits and cottontails. Beavers burrow in sandy streambanks. In the spring a carpet of wildflowers transforms the desert for a while. It is easier to imagine Navajo or Anasazi inhabitants—their rock writings can be found here—than it is to conjure up visions of the cowhands, settlers, bandits and soldiers who passed through. Still, there are a few faint signs of man's presence. Turnbow Cabin, on the banks of Salt Creek near Delicate Arch, dates from the 1880s, when a Civil War veteran from Ohio named John Wolfe squatted on the land with his son. And later ranchers and then prospectors looking for uranium and geologists scouting for oil and natural gas left their faint marks too—a few trails across the stony ground. Arches was a national monument until 1971, when it became a national park; but its climate and geography had already done a respectable job of protecting it from development.

Pine Tree Arch.

The grandeur of Delicate Arch at sunset.

1.

1. Detail of the top of Delicate Arch.

2. An isolated remnant of a bygone year, Delicate Arch.

1. Base of North Window.

2. Skyline Arch, now half the size it was in the 1940s.

3. Landscape Arch, one of the most remarkable, with a span of 291 feet.

2.

1.

2.

3.

1. *The Windows as seen through Turret Arch.*

2. *The famous Balance Rock.*

3. *Pine Tree Arch in the warm, late afternoon light.*

1. *Turret Arch.*

2. *Silhouette of Sand Dune Arch.*

3. *Dramatic overview of exposed firs from Fiery Furnace overlook.*

1.

2.

3.

1. Delicate Arch Trail with the La Sal Mountains in the background.

2. A young doe near Delicate Arch.

3. Majestic rock outcroppings at The Garden of Eden.

1.

2.

3.

BIG BEND
NATIONAL PARK

Texas

America's Empty Quarter

IF IT'S TEXAS, it must be big. And so it is—1,000 square miles of unusual geological features, moody vistas, and mountain and desert wilderness, tucked into that broad bend of the Rio Grande that pokes down from southwest Texas into Mexico's northern Sierra Madre. In the local Spanish, it is the *gran comba*, part of the great Chihuahuan desert, and it cradles a number of natural anomalies that make this area remarkable.

To the present-day visitor, the most noticeable is the river itself. The Rio Grande makes a narrow ribbon of green, like a linear oasis, through what seems to be mere lifeless scrub and sand and rock, and attracts wildlife to itself like a magnet. From the eastern to the western boundary of Big Bend Park, the river flows more than 100 miles and has cut three majestic canyons into the country rock, called Boquillas, Mariscal and Santa Elena. The latter is the most spectacular—a 15-mile crevasse through the desert that reaches down as much as 1,500 feet between sheer walls of stone. To hike the trail to the bottom, which follows a sometimes precarious ledge, or to run the river in a rubber raft, is to travel through geologic time into an earlier age.

The rock is sedimentary, limestones and sandstones, and the erosion and sculpting is occasionally intricate, occasionally mammoth, but always captivating. The great glaciers of the last Ice Age, approximately 10,000 years ago, never reached this far south. This kind of delicate chiseling, which may leave delicate swirls in apparently unyielding rock, can only be formed by water. The Rio Grande is an especially efficient cutting tool; its current carries so much sediment that at times it can be heard whispering against the skin of an aluminum boat as if it were a liquid abrasive.

The Chisos Mountains, in the center of Big Bend, are home to a number of rare or unique species of animals. The Carmen deer, a race of whitetails, exists only here and across the border in Mexico's Sierra del Carmen. Whitetail deer are no more desert creatures than are Douglas fir trees, but both are native to Big Bend. They were probably marooned here in the high country when the glaciers retreated, taking their more temperate weather with them, and the lowlands turned into hot desert.

With peaks that reach to more than 7,000 feet, the mountains rise like green islands out of the ochre plains. The timber line occurs at about 4,000 feet, but it is a reverse line—the larger trees can only survive *above* that mark, where the climate is cooler and more moist. The progression is from grasslands to low green shrubs and then taller, leafier bushes such as sumac, bee bush and Texas madrone. Next come the stunted oak trees, acacias and piñon pines. The climax comes with ponderosa pines,

Douglas fir, quaking aspen, cypress and even maple trees. The high Chisos forest is the southern extremity of the American range of some of these species, which were common throughout the entire region thousands of years ago, when the glaciers that reached into Colorado kept temperatures lower than they are now. Now, the Chisos are also the northern tip of the range of the drooping juniper, which is common in Mexico but found in the United States only in Big Bend. Like many American national parks, Big Bend is the crossroads, or overlap, of a variety of ecosystems.

Below the tree line lives the sagebrush, desert willow, mesquite, pricklypear, yucca and lechuguilla, which resembles a thicket of daggers sprouting from the ground. There are many different kinds of cactus too, the quintessential water-misers of the American Southwest. The most remarkably adapted desert plant, however, is the creosotebush, which guards its turf—and thus its own little watershed—by producing a poison that keeps other plants, potential competitors for water and nutrients, from growing nearby. A patch of these bushes, the most common in Big Bend, looks as though it was planted by a gardener with a passion for even spacing and regular weeding, but there is nothing artificial about it. The name comes from the sticky resin the plant exudes over its leaves, to slow down the evapotranspiration of moisture into the air. (The locals say that every plant in the desert either "sticks, stings or stinks.")

To go from timber line to desert floor is to go from whitetail deer to jackrabbits, roadrunners, tarantulas, rattlesnakes and kangaroo rats. But there are more anomalies in Big Bend's lowlands too, for example, the beavers that live along the Rio Grande. They find enough cottonwood trees and willows to eat, but not enough to build northern-style lodges, so these warmwater beavers live in burrows in the riverbanks. There are killdeer and sandpipers on the river too, also more northerly animals. Incredibly, more than 400 different kinds of birds have been identified in Big Bend—again, an unusual mix of northern species reaching southward and southern birds extending northward, plus many more that pass through on annual cross-continental migrations.

AS DESERTS GO, the Chihuahuan is greener and less arid than most—though visitors are still cautioned to check their fuel and water reserves early and often—and much of the rainfall it gets arrives in the summer growing season. To see Big Bend after the first good spring rains, in March or April, is to gain an entirely new appreciation for desert. With the intensity of organisms that must do business in a short growing season, every desiccated cactus and dried-out-seeming shrub, every spindly stalk that is in actuality a wildflower, bursts forth in an astonishing array of delicate blossoms. Every hue of red, yellow, lavender and white blooms across the "dead" ground, and the air is filled with their perfume.

Compared to better-known and more populated parks such as Yosemite or Yellowstone, Big Bend seems completely undeveloped, and this is another of its anomalies. It is one of the "forgotten" parks, apparently on no motorhome-owners' club routes. To "discover" it, then, with its comparatively few amenities and rustic campgrounds (which, being relatively few, nevertheless do fill up every year), is all the more rewarding. It was originally called Big Bend National *Primeval* Park, and the name still fits.

Following the lead of Waterton/Glacier Park, at the opposite border of the United States, Big Bend might someday become the second International Peace Park on earth—if the Mexican government could see its way clear to establishing a matching park on their side of the Rio Grande. For a few years after the American park was signed into existence, in 1944, the National Park Service seemed optimistic that this would occur, but momentum has died down and there is little talk of such an agreement now. Perhaps more time has to pass—for more than 400 years bandits, soldiers, missionaries, explorers, lawmen, thieves and Indians crossed and re-crossed the border through Big Bend country, often with less than honorable intentions. The last overtly hostile action between Mexico and the United States took place only in 1916, when a band of revolutionary guerrillas invaded the United States by way of Big Bend. And today illegal immigrants and smugglers of everything from drugs to parakeets and candelilla wax use the river and its convoluted canyons to do their business in secret. Perhaps the time simply isn't right yet for a "peace" park on this border.

1. *Goat Mountains with cactus in the foreground.*

2. *Cactus.*

3. *View along Window Trail.*

1.

2.

3.

1. *Chisos Mountains.*

2. *Detail of rock formation on the Window Trail.*

3. *View along Window Trail.*

1.

2.

3.

1. Rock pool in Big Bend.

2. Castolon Peak as seen from the road between Ruff Canyon and Castolon.

3. Rock formation on road between Tuff Canyon and Castolon.

1.

2.

3.

1. Castolon Peak.

2. Cactus flowers.

3. Castolon Peak.

1. *Bison pictograph.*

2. *The dry, cracked riverbed of the Rio Grande River seen from Hot Springs Trail.*

3. *Detail of the dry riverbed of the Rio Grande River in Santa Helena Canyon.*

1.

2.

3.

View of the Rio Grande River from Boquillas Canyon Trail.

1.

1. The purple and white flowers of cenizo sage brighten the trails in Big Bend National Park.

2. Rio Grande riverbed.

3. The Boquillas Canyon overlook.

2.

3.

1. The Chisos Mountains as seen from the Basin Section.

2. Shadows lengthen as the sun sets at Boquillas Canyon.

3. A brilliant sunset at Sotol Vista overlook.

1.

2.

3.

A breathtaking view from Lost Mine Trail.

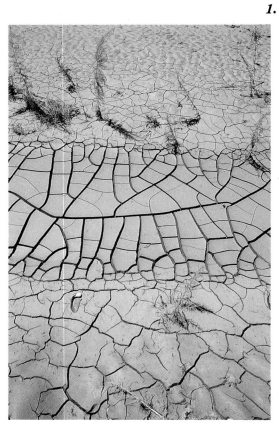

1. The dry, cracked riverbed of the Rio Grande River forms interesting patterns in the Santa Helena Canyon.

2. Visible in the background of this desolate scene is Castolon Peak.

3. An alert deer rests in the cool shade of the trees.

BRYCE CANYON NATIONAL PARK

Utah

A Carved Fantasyland

EBENEZER BRYCE, the Mormon who settled on this peculiar land in 1874, gave the canyon its name and its reputation. He called it "a hell of a place to lose a cow!" He was here at the behest of the Mormon Church, up in Salt Lake City; the elders hoped to establish cotton plantations here and so, improbable as it sounds, dubbed the area Dixie Land. Bryce and the other pioneers found that it would take far more than a wishful name-change to turn bare rock into an oasis, and he gave it up after five years.

The name is actually a misnomer; there is no Bryce canyon—but there are small canyons, and hollows and passes and gaps, throughout the park. Bryce is not one big ravine with a river running through it. It is, however, a series of amphitheaters, natural stone bowls, carved into the edge of Utah's Paunsaugunt Plateau. From certain vantage points, the amphitheaters seem to be packed shoulder-to-shoulder with concert-goers—the "red rocks standing like men" of the original Paiute Indian name. These marvelous stone flutes and towers vary from delicate lavenders and pinks to bold reds and purples, and the hues shift almost from minute to minute as sun and clouds play across them. Snow lying lightly on the rims and ramparts sometimes looks like frosting on a fantastic layer cake. With names like Queen's Castle, Wall of Windows, Thor's Hammer, the Camel and the Wiseman, the formations may resemble minarets and pagodas, or fairy-tale creatures petrified in their tracks by the magic that created Bryce.

Between Bryce Canyon and the Grand Canyon is the so-called Grand Staircase, a series of north-facing cliffs that are each the exposed end of a thick layer of rock. These layers were originally horizontal beds of sediment deposited in ancient seas and lakes; the steps of the Staircase were formed when the beds were tilted up and fractured. The bottom layer, and thus the oldest formation of the Staircase to emerge from the earth, is the Kaibab Plateau; its southern edge forms the North Rim of the Grand Canyon. At the other end, the youngest "step" is the Pink Cliffs sandstone (at merely 50 million years of age, it is about 200 million years newer than the Kaibab). The Bryce amphitheaters are cut into the Pink Cliffs.

At Bryce, the terrain is steep and the stone is soft, and rain and snow are surprisingly common; erosion is so rapid that topsoil has little chance to form. A few species of hardy evergreens and grasses—and the mule deer, coyotes and other wild animals that shelter in them—thrive here, but man has never been able to tame these badlands with crops or domestic animals. They will be free to go on, forever changing.

1.

1. *Unusual rock formations abound at Bryce Canyon National Park.*

1. *Agua Canyon.*

2. *Sunset at Bryce Point.*

1.

2.

1.

2.

1. The force of erosion forms intricate cuts in these rock formations.

2. In some areas of Bryce Canyon National Park these impressive Hoodoos can reach up to 200 feet.

1. Travel made easier with a passageway cut into the rock on the famous Navajo/Queens Garden Trail.

2. The Hoodoos are aglow with the setting sun at Bryce Point.

1.

2.

Inspiration Point.

1. The red and orange colors visible in this rock formation are caused by iron oxide.

2. Paria view at sunset.

1.

2.

1. *Fairyland Point.*

2. *A panoramic view of Rainbow Point.*

3. *Intricate Hoodoos along the Navajo/Queens Garden Trail.*

1.

2.

3.

A doorway cut into the rock along the Navajo/Queens Garden Trail.

Sunrise at Bryce Point.

CANYONLANDS NATIONAL PARK
Utah

Wilderness of Rock

WHERE THE GREEN and the great Colorado rivers come together in southeastern Utah is another of the Southwest's geological fantasias, this one known—since 1964, when Congress set it aside in the public trust—as Canyonlands National Park. The park is more than 500 square miles of billiard-table-flat, ochre-red sedimentary rock, much of which has been cut and etched into uncountable canyons, mesas, buttes, rock windows, towers and other notable shapes.

On the three sides of the river junction are the three distinctly different zones of the park, known as the Maze, the Needles and Island in the Sky. The Maze, west of the confluence, is named for the "thirty-square-mile puzzle in sandstone" at its heart. This is badlands country at its worst—or best: a daunting, desert-dry, and seemingly impenetrable wilderness, a three-dimensional confusion that dips below grade as much as 600 feet. From some vantage points, the horizontal striations on the buttes (the layers of different rock) make everything blend together like an optical illusion, or a particularly effective stone camouflage.

In the vee of the two rivers lies Island in the Sky, the wide mesa that serves as Canyonlands' observation post. From here, it is as if the viewer is looking into a mini Grand Canyon, with broad stone benches falling away down to the two rivers at the very bottom. Lifting his eyes to the horizon, the visitor sees a splendid landscape stretching across 100 miles of flat-topped buttes and towers, their cliffs dropping into shadow beneath. Arcing around the horizon from east to southwest, three mountain ranges outside the park lift their far—and often snow-capped—peaks to the wide-open blue sky. Island in the Sky is an arid place. The vegetation is sparse and gnarly, desert pastures of rice grass edged with clumps of stunted piñon pines and junipers. The most unusual feature on the Island mesa itself is a large crater called, incongruously, Upheaval Dome.

The Needles area of Canyonlands, east of the Colorado River, takes its name from the countless spires of bare rock that clump together as if they were a carpet of quills. And, as does nearby Arches National Park, Needles has many natural stone bridges and windows hidden away in its back country. Bands of Anasazi Indians lived among the Needles, part of the highly civilized race of "Ancient Ones" who built the great pueblos of Mesa Verde and Chaco Canyon. They vanished from the Southwest centuries ago. Many of their stone dwellings and storehouses remain, well preserved, and their petroglyphs and pictographs decorate the cliff walls.

1.

1. The Needles section.

2. Evening begins to fall in the Needles section.

1. A magnificent view of the Needles section from the road.

2. Travel to the Needles is made possible by a road located outside the Canyonlands National Park.

2.

1.

2.

1.

2.

1. Bushes and trees grow freely among the rock formations in the Needles section.

This natural rock sculpture can be found along the Pothole Point Trail.

2. One of the many unique rock formations in the Needles section.

1. *Sunset in the Needles section.*

2. *The Island in the Sky section of Canyonlands National Park is visible from the Mesa Arches.*

3. *A view of the Canyonlands from Dead Horse Point State Park.*

1.

2.

3.

*The sun turns the rocks afire at
Grandview Point overlook.*

1. *Green River overlook in the Island in the Sky region.*

2. *A new day dawns in the Island in the Sky section.*

3. *A formidable view from the Mesa Arch Trail.*

1.

2.

3.

1. *Rocks, worn away by the elements, exhibit some unusual formations in Big Spring Canyon.*

2. *Elephant Hill is located in the Needles section.*

3. *An antelope grazes in the shadow of the La Sal Mountains.*

1.

2.

3.

1. *Newspaper Rock.*

2. *Indian ruins such as this one can be discovered on the Roadside Ruin Trail.*

2.

CAPITOL REEF NATIONAL PARK

Utah

Along the Waterpocket Fold

IT REALLY ISN'T a reef, but this enormous berm of twisted and water-eaten sandstones that winds gently across south-central Utah for almost 100 miles certainly resembles one. The Waterpocket Fold, as it is known to geologists and geographers, is the meager—but still impressive—remnant of a giant wrinkle in the earth's crust. It is also an edge of the great Colorado Plateau, and it was born when those thick layers of sedimentary rock were slowly lifted up by forces within the earth's core. Very gradually, the upper layers of the ancient Fold were worn away.

The present-day Fold is only the exposed edges of some of those up-tilted rock strata. Its name comes from the small natural basins that trap rain water and snowmelt. Waterpockets have meant life for many desert animals, man included, but ironically water sitting atop friable rock in such a climate of temperature extremes usually means "death" for the stone—if freezing-and-thawing, cracking and erosion can be called death. Throughout the red-rock country of Utah and the Southwest, the marvelous geological formations are constantly changing.

Capitol Reef—"capitol" because of the rounded white peaks in the Navajo Sandstone—is a particularly scenic spur of the great Fold, a giant's garden of colorful cliffs and domes, craggy castle formations, stone spires and arches. They bear evocative names such as Egyptian Temple, Golden Throne and the Sleeping Rainbow formation. Long a national monument, Capitol Reef became the core of this long, slender national park only in 1971. It is little known even in Utah, and it is far off the beaten path of the motor homes that congregate in America's major parks every summer. Only one paved road cuts through the park. But the visitor who enters is rewarded with a varied and ancient terrain seemingly spared the attentions of modern man. Most visitors see only the Scenic Drive, a 25-mile gravel road that loops through the park, but many spectacular areas are accessible only to four-wheel-drive vehicles.

The Fremont River is the park's lifeblood. The thickets of cottonwood, willows and ash along its banks have attracted animals for centuries. People also came to this green oasis. They ranged from the archaic Fremont Culture, contemporaries of the Anasazi, who lived farther south, to modern-day Mormon farmers who established the small town of Fruita. It's a ghost town now; the citizenry began to leave after the Reef became a national monument in 1937, which closed off future development. They left behind log cabins and a prim schoolhouse, and their orchards still flourish unattended. Deer, coyotes, jackrabbits and yellow-bellied marmots inhabit Fruita now.

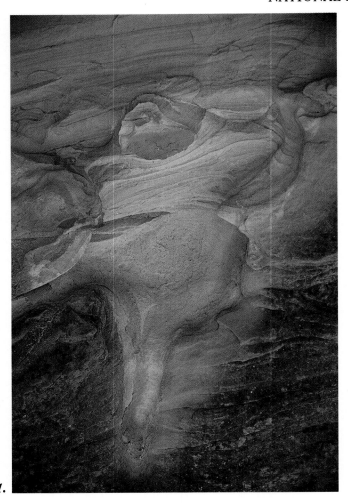

1.

1. *The form and color of this natural rock petroglyph give the appearance of a dancer.*

2. *Fremont petroglyphs.*

The variations of color in this massive rock wall give the appearance of a tapestry.

2.

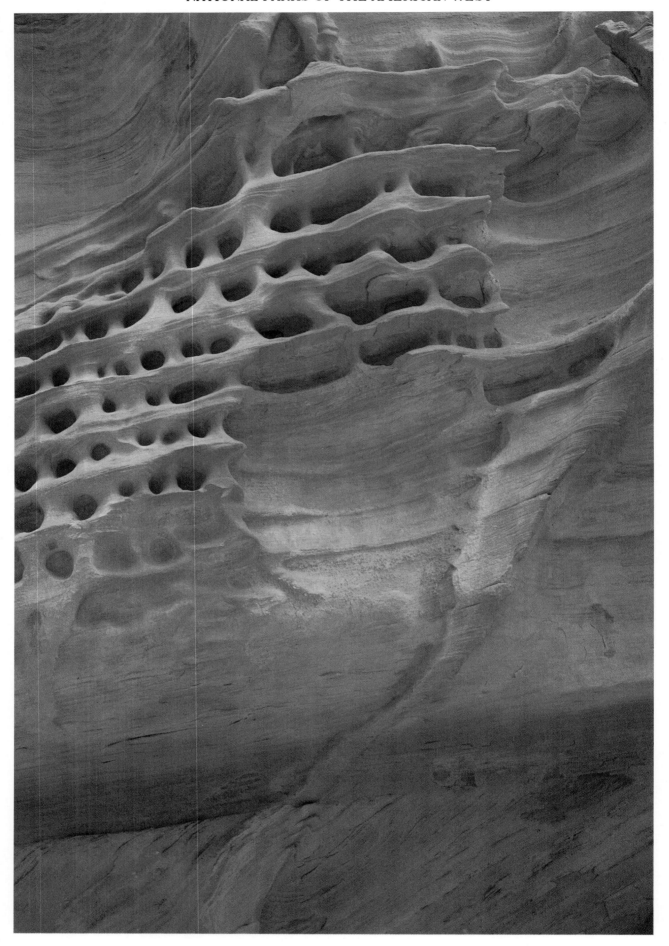

Detail of Honeycomb Rock.

1. *A striking overview of Honeycomb Rock.*

2. *The Capitol Gorge.*

1.

2.

1.

2.

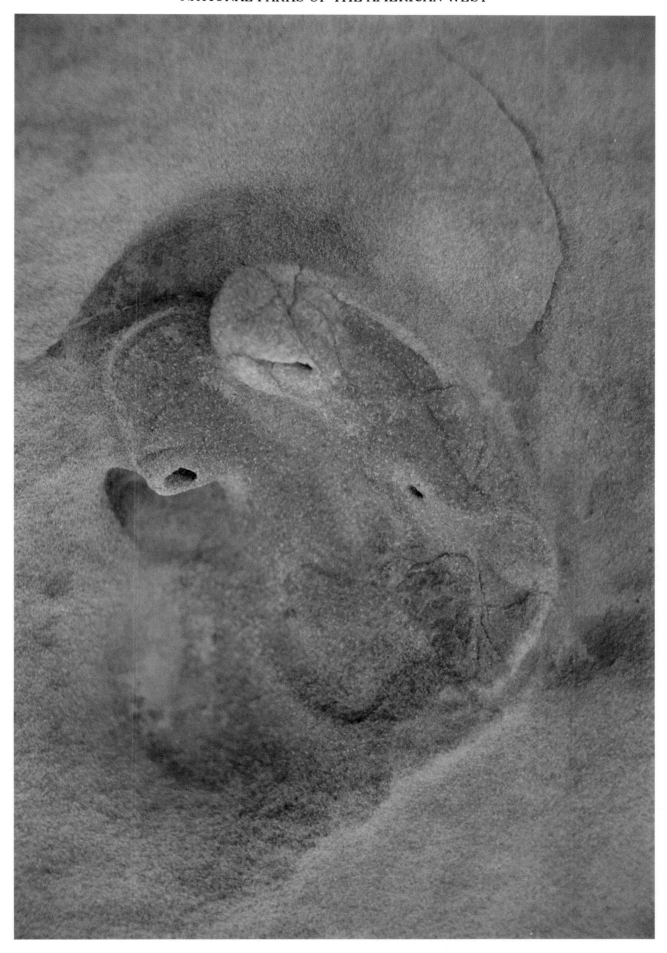

1. *A scenic drive enables visitors to witness some of the most fascinating rock formations nature has ever created.*

2. The Egyptian Temple.

Detail of an unusual sandstone formation.

1. *The Goosenecks.*

2. *An abundance of fallen rocks can be seen during the Scenic Drive.*

1.

2.

CARLSBAD CAVERNS NATIONAL PARK

New Mexico

Unknown, Unseen Wonders

THE MOST FAMOUS CAVES on earth were dismissed for decades as fanciful inventions, stories made up by rural publicity-seekers. But today, long after the tales were proven true, the full extent of these fantastic structures is still unknown. The entrances of more than 70 caves lie within Carlsbad Park's 47,000 acres, but some still are not mapped. Even Carlsbad, the biggest of them, has been explored only to an extent of about 20 miles, though spelunkers continue to push the boundaries—and no one knows how far the tunnels really go.

A cowboy named Jim White gets most of the credit for discovering Carlsbad Caverns, though of course the Indians knew of them centuries before. Settlers in southeastern New Mexico in the 19th century were attracted to the caves by the immense numbers of bats that poured out like plumes of smoke every summer evening. It didn't take long to discover the equally huge deposits of bat guano inside, and that led to a small-scale "gold rush" as people staked claims and began to mine the phosphates for fertilizer. In 20 years, more than 100,00 tons of guano were taken out of Carlsbad. Jim White was one of the miners, but he was more interested in the cave than in its bounty; he explored it and tried to convince others of what he had seen. Finally, in 1915, he persuaded a photographer named Ray Davis to accompany him, and his pictures did the trick. White then found himself in much demand as a guide, and the bucket-and-windlass that had been used to lift guano out of the depths became a tourist elevator.

In 1923 the Department of the Interior sent an investigator to debunk once and for all this hoax. Instead, his report led to the cavern's designation as a national monument that same year, and in 1930 it became a national park. Fittingly, White became the park's first chief ranger, and was able to continue his explorations for years.

The limestone walls of the cavern contain imbedded marine fossils that are 200 million years old—the first clue to its formation. It was once the Capitan Reef, 400 miles long, in a prehistoric sea. As the reef calcified and the waters evaporated, sediments were laid down on top. Cracks and erosion began to admit rain water. Combining with carbon dioxide and ancient salts, the water formed pockets of acid, which—over 200 million more years—dissolved out the stupendous chambers. Almost the same process forms the myriad extraordinary formations that decorate the caves. Individual drops of acidic water, penetrating the cavern roofs, deposit their minuscule load of calcite wherever they fall—and bit by bit grow fantastic stone stalagmites and stalactites, columns, draperies, soda straws, popcorn, cave pearls, helictites and lily pads.

Strata in various sizes, shapes and colors have been forming for hundreds of years at Carlsbad Caverns National Park.

CRATER LAKE NATIONAL PARK
Oregon

Big Blue

CRATER LAKE, which plunges to 1,932 feet, is the deepest body of water in North America. It also reflects the world's deepest, bluest blue. When its surface is unruffled, gazing down into the lake from the surrounding rim can be confusing, almost mystifying; it is a thing without beginning or end. A century ago, the Klamath Indians regarded it as a holy place, and their shamans instructed them to avoid it. The taboo extended to others too—for decades, the Indians told no white man about the lake's existence. It wasn't until 1853 that a group of prospectors, combing the mountains for a legendary "lost" gold mine, stumbled across its cerulean majesty.

The native people's concept of the lake may have been rooted in their minds by the way it was formed, for their ancestors were probably around to witness its explosive birth. "Crater" Lake is just that; but it is not a meteor-impact crater, as its symmetric roundness and abrupt rim seems to suggest. The real clues are its depth—an average of 1,500 feet, plus the height of the rim above water—along with its location within the volcanically active Cascade Range, and the presence of conical Wizard Island on its west side. This crater is essentially the reverse of a volcano—a mountain turned inside out. Wizard Island is the original volcano's "offspring," a second, and smaller, cone.

Five hundred thousand years ago, the first cone of a volcano now named Mount Mazama began to form on the site. Eventually, more vents opened up, and increasing heat and pressure from beneath caused fractures and local slumping on the by-now large dome. Finally, only about 7,000 years ago, with the catastrophic suddenness we saw very recently at nearby Mount St. Helens, Mazama exploded. So much material was blasted out of the earth that the mountain's remnant shards collapsed inward and down. Ash fell 6 inches deep over an area of 5,000 square miles.

The resulting crater, called a caldera, eventually began to fill with rain and snow—after it cooled down and after further volcanic activity, which built Wizard Island, closed off the floor of the crater. For centuries now, the magma beneath has been quiet. Neither streams nor springs feed or drain the lake, but precipitation, the heavy snow and rain that the Cascade Mountains pull out of the wet Pacific air streaming eastward, and evaporation have balanced each other off. The lake level is stable to within 3 feet per year. The water is almost sterile, and the trout and salmon (exotics introduced around the turn of the century) that remain must forage near the surface for wind-blown terrestrial insects. Finally, Crater Lake almost never freezes over, because this massive volume of water stores enough summer heat to keep ice at bay.

The stark rock walls of Crater Lake are reflected in the icy-blue surface of the water.

Because of its shape, this tiny rock islet is known as Phantom Ship.

1. The Phantom Ship appears to be but a pebble when compared to the surrounding rock walls of Crater Lake.

2. Crater Lake.

1.

2.

1.

2.

1. *The blueness of the water acts as a beautiful backdrop for this interesting rock formation found at the edge of Crater Lake.*

2. *Wizard Island, a volcanic cone, rises out of the blue depth of Crater Lake.*

Lush greenery abounds near Vidae Falls.

The Pinnacles.

WATERTON/GLACIER INTERNATIONAL PEACE PARK

Alberta-Montana

A Park Bridging Two Nations

DIVIDED only by a manmade slash through the forest that overlaps two adjoining political systems, Canada's Waterton Lakes National Park, which lies in Alberta, and Montana's Glacier National Park, in the United States, are in fact—geologically and ecologically—extensions of one another.

Physically, this vast, high-mountain region was shaped by the unimaginable earth-sculpting power of great sheets of ice. Administratively, as a permanent refuge for wildlife and sanctuary of wilderness, Waterton/Glacier was formed in 1932 by the concerted actions of Canada's Parliament and the United States Congress. Waterton Lakes National Park had been set aside in 1895; south of the border, Glacier came into being just 15 years later. The instigators of their union, a unique arrangement, were the Rotary Clubs on both sides of the 49th parallel, the United States-Canadian line (itself formally adopted only in 1818).

As the first International Peace Park, Waterton/Glacier symbolizes the friendship and cultural bond between two neighbor nations. On the scientific end, the United Nations Educational, Scientific & Cultural Organization(UNESCO), designated the park to be earth's first International Biosphere Reserve, to help "preserve genetic diversity and to explore the relationships between the parks and the neighboring lands and peoples."

These are lofty goals, and ones that would seem to demand an equally grand setting. Waterton/Glacier is up to it, however. It is 1 million acres of pristine lakes, golden prairie, deep green conifer forest, meadows of short-lived alpine flowers and hundreds of towering crags. These elements combine for miles of stunning, sweeping vistas. The sudden uplift of the mountains brings together varied terrains, and their inhabitants, that aren't normally seen in such close proximity. There are plenty of geologic oddities too. Naturalist-explorer George Grinnell was the first to determine that a drop of rain falling on 8,011-foot Triple-Divide Peak (in the southeast quadrant of the park) could flow to the Pacific Ocean, the Gulf of Mexico or Hudson's Bay. He dubbed it the "crown of the continent." And the Garden Wall is a perfect example of a glacial arête, the vertical remnant of a mountain ridge that was carved to a knife-edge by ice sheets moving slowly past on both sides, leaving exposed millions of years for the geologic record.

Although the park has four peaks that top 10,000 feet (and many more that come close), and despite its northern latitude and its exposure to weather moving down from the Canadian Arctic, the glaciers that shaped the park and gave it its name have been melting for centuries, exposing more and more of their scoured, U-shaped valleys. The largest, Grinnell Glacier, now about 275 acres, is only about half what it was when Grinnell—one of America's foremost naturalists and explorers at the turn of the last century—set foot on it 100 years ago. There are still, however, about 50 small glaciers and permanent snowfields within the park, and many are accessible to those who will leave their cars and campers for even an afternoon. (The pleasure of a snowball fight on a still, hot, high-altitude day is something that has to be experienced.)

Man's intrusions cover only about 7 percent of the park—including, perhaps ironically, three luxurious hotels (built by the Great Northern Railway in the early 1900s to attract train-travelling tourists) along with the more than 700 miles of hiking trails. A few of these manmade things, such as the renowned and spectacular Going-to-the-Sun Road, may even add to rather than subtract from the park's grandeur. On the nature scene, some 60 native mammal species reside here, and 250 kinds of birds, and more than 1,000 different plants. There is a relatively large and stable population of grizzly bears, and the park is one of a handful of places where timber wolves still exist in the Lower 48.

Thanks largely to the protection afforded by its remoteness, its hard, long winters, and its sheer size, Glacier/Waterton today is still very much the Rocky Mountains that the 19th-century trappers and mountain men. Beautiful and grand as it is, modern man still ventures afield at his or her own risk—the weather can be extreme; and the park sees about two bear maulings a year. Five people were killed by bears between 1977 and 1989, and park officials go to great lengths to try to educate visitors about the problem. There are warning signs, lectures and brochures that point out that bear attacks can almost always be avoided if people use common sense. In fact, for every hiker who sees a bear, black or grizzly—and every visitor wants that unforgettable thrill— probably hundreds more have passed within shouting distance of one that chose to lay low in the brush. To remove the risk by eradicating the bears, which a few people propose every time an "incident" occurs, here or in Yellowstone, would be to peel away an important layer of what makes North American wilderness truly wild. We have spent two centuries doing just that, taming our wild lands; today, fortunately, public sentiment has swung the other way, to a new respect for the earth, and the mere existence of free-roaming grizzly bears helps keep us humble.

RANGERS, wardens, administrators, politicians and citizens on both sides of the border want to keep Waterton/Glacier the way it has been. But, as always and everywhere, threats are encroaching. Often the people behind them, such as hunting outfitters and tour operators, aren't even aware that they are threats. The park is surrounded by government land, mostly the huge Flathead national (in the United States) and provincial (in Canada) forests and, on the east, by the Blackfeet and Blood Indian Reservations. Nevertheless, within a few miles of the park's boundaries, crews are detonating charges in seismic surveys for oil; timber companies are clear-cutting irretrievable old-growth forest; and developers are building, or applying to build, vacation homes and their roads, utility lines and septic systems. Incredibly, just north of the park lies a huge Shell Canada natural-gas drilling and refining plant, and at least twice so far escaping hydrogen sulfide gas has forced emergency evacuations of the nearby town of Twin Butte, Alberta. For more than a decade, Canadian and American conservationists and citizens alike have been fighting a plan to create an enormous open-pit coal mine, and its workers' town, on the British Columbia side of the Continental Divide, just west of the Waterton side of the park.

Development pressure along the park's edges will continue as long as there is a use for coal, oil, natural gas, timber, gold, water and so on. But if there was ever a natural preserve that, on the face of it, was well protected, this might be it. With the environmental guardians of two enlightened countries watching over it, and politicians and citizens gathering there every July to commemorate the United States-Canada Days of Peace and Friendship, Waterton/Glacier, the International Peace Park, should have a secure future. All that needs to be accomplished within the park is to let the clearcut that marks the border grow back.

The first rays of sunlight brighten a valley of clouds at Logan Pass.

1.

1. *Whether in the grass, trees or bushes, wildlife aboundst at Glacier National Park.*

2. *Lunch Creek.*

3. *Clouds envelope Logan Pass, surrounding it in mystery.*

2.

3.

1. An inquisitive marmot appears completely at home before the camera.

2. A mountain goat practicing some fancy footwork for his visitors.

3. This chipmunk doesn't seem to mind eating his greens for dinner!

1.

2.

3.

As the moon rises, a feeling of peace and tranquillity reigns over St. Mary Lake.

1. *Another day is over as the sun sets at Lake MacDonald.*

2. *Swiftcurrent Lake reflects the beauty of the surrounding land in the many glacier section.*

1.

2.

1.

2.

3.

1. *The beauty of nature is clearly visible in this view from the trail to Hidden Lake at dusk.*

2. *Sundrift Gorge.*

3. *Concealed in the mountain ranges, Hidden Lake flows undisturbed.*

Early morning mist is burned away when the sun rises over Sherburne Lake.

Panoramic view of Bowman Lake.

1. *Out of the smooth surface of St. Mary Lake rises Wild Goose Island.*

2. *A view of St. Mary Lake from Sun Point.*

1.

2.

1. *Lower Two Medecine Lake.*

2. *The scent and sight of wildflowers envelope Sherburne Lake.*

3. *One of the impressive views of rock formations that can be seen along the Going-to-the-Sun Road.*

1.

2.

3.

GRAND CANYON NATIONAL PARK

Arizona

A Land to Humble the Soul

THE TERM 'GRAND' falls far short of depicting this indescribable cleft in the earth, the deepest, longest and by far the most spectacular feature along the Colorado River's 1,400-mile run. To stand on one of the many lookout points and stare into and across the Canyon is to view the bones of the earth. No photograph can completely capture the spectacle, or even do it justice. Americans, accustomed to wide-open spaces, are often struck dumb. European visitors—to whom the United States seems incredibly vast and untouched to begin with—sometimes burst into tears. The senses reel.

Colossal and still though the Canyon is, it is not static. Its Park Service guardians have set the stage as well as anyone can: "The scene continually changes as light plays off the rocks and clouds, creating shadows and contrasts. The world seems larger here, with sunrises, sunsets and storms taking on an added dimension to match the landscape. The permutations are unceasing, and the moods are without end. This is a land to humble the soul."

Congress voted Grand Canyon National Park into existence in 1919. It spans only some 75 miles, from the Lake Mead Recreational Area on the west to the Navajo Indian Reservation in the Painted Desert on the east. The Canyon, however, is 277 miles long. It is also a mile deep in places, and from 1 to 14 miles wide from rim to rim; more than 1,000 square miles in total area. The multicolored striations in the Canyon walls are the seemingly endless layers of different rock formations that have been deposited, by sedimentation or volcanism, over the ages and then exposed by the relentless down-cutting of the river. These walls are a textbook of the southwestern American geological record, exposing rock as old as 1.7 billion years. Unlike many rivers in the glaciated north, which were changed by—or born during—the Ice Age, the present-day Colorado River has flowed along largely the same path since the beginning of the Pliocene. The Canyon was cut without the cataclysmic aid of a great glacier; simply, as geologic forces pushed the plateau upwards, the river's current wore down into its limestone, sandstone and shale, down to the granite beneath. To gouge such a crevasse into the desert has taken 5 million to 7 million years—and the process continues.

There is still an Indian village within the Canyon, in the Havasupai Reservation on the western edge of the park. Supplies are brought in by mule train, and visitors to Supai, enchanted by the relaxed pace and the blue-green travertine pools of the Havasu River, feel that they have entered a magic kingdom. It is but a remnant of earlier civilizations. In these side canyons and tributaries as well as along the main stream, more than 700 pueblo sites have been found in the Grand Canyon; most were occupied about 1,000 years ago.

TO A VISITOR on the rim, newly arrived from Yellowstone or Glacier, the Grand Canyon at first seems desolate of wildlife, truly a "painted desert." But to the visitor who climbs down in and gets a closer glimpse, animal and plant life is abundant. Deer, burros and wild horses roam the park, preyed on by coyotes, bobcats and a handful of mountain lions. Desert animals from rattlesnakes to spiders are common. From the floor of the Canyon near Canyon Village to the tops of the San Francisco Peaks, in the Kaibab National Forest southeast of the park, it is only 60 miles horizontally and 11,000 feet vertically—but in terms of the vegetation that grows in those zones, the distance is the same as between subtropical and Arctic latitudes. And within the Canyon there is such a variety of ecological zones that to see something similar on the outside would require hiking from Canada to Mexico.

Similar extremes can be found everywhere in the Grand Canyon. Visitors who take the two-day round-trip hike down the Bright Angel Trail, near park headquarters, often find themselves sweltering in the heat at the river's edge—while at the Canyon rim, only 10 miles back and 4,400 feet up, they are chilly in sweaters and windbreakers.

The Colorado River is also a study in contrasts and extremes. The best way to see and appreciate the Canyon—truly to immerse oneself in its incomprehensible vastness—is from the bottom, from a riverboat. But the Colorado alternates between miles of glassy smooth, tranquil flows to roaring descents through immense white-water cataracts of unimaginable hydraulic power. Float trips down the Colorado were dangerously impractical until the advent of large, rugged, flexible and essentially unsinkable inflatable rafts, and now the trip is alternately serene and merely thrilling, and quite safe.

Only in the grip of the Canyon's rapids is it possible to get some real appreciation for the effort, and sheer bravery, of John Wesley Powell and his crew. They were the first white men—probably the first of all men—to run the Canyon in boats and live to tell about it. They did it long before the river was tamed by dams, and they did it blind— that is, with no knowledge of what lay before them. Powell, the geologist and anthropologist whose name has been given to a number of landmarks on the Colorado Plateau, rose from private to major in the Union Army during the Civil War. Although he lost an arm at the Battle of Shiloh, he went on to spend years exploring the Intermountain West. His descent of the Colorado River, called the "last important exploration within the continental United States," was his crowning achievement. In May 1869, Powell and 10 men pushed off on the Green River, a tributary in Wyoming, in four small wooden boats. Three months later, after many harrowing near-misses and significant hardships (four men left the expedition en route), they had successfully traversed 900 miles of the river.

The climax of the trip was the Grand Canyon. Powell, in his classic *Exploration of the Colorado River of the West and Its Tributaries*, wrote at the beginning of the Canyon: "We are now ready to start on our way down the Great Unknown. Our boats, tied to a common stake, are chafing each other, as they are tossed by the fretful river. They ride high and buoyant, for their loads are lighter than we could desire. We have but a month's rations remaining . . . . We have an unknown distance yet to run; an unknown river yet to explore. What falls there are, we know not; what walls rise over the river, we know not. Ah well! We may conjecture many things. The men talk as cheerfully as ever; jests are bandied about freely this morning; but to me the cheer is somber and the jests are ghastly."

Almost equally remarkable is the fact that the Grand Canyon had never been walked from end to end, at least in white history, until the mid-1960s. Colin Fletcher, the writer/hiker, did it in two months, with three airdrops to resupply along the way. His account of the trip, *The Man Who Walked Through Time*, is one of the best appreciations of the Canyon ever written.

Another was uttered by President Teddy Roosevelt, who declared the Grand Canyon a national monument in 1908. He stood on the rim and said, "Leave it as it is. You cannot improve on it. The ages have been at work on it, and man can only mar it."

The sun sets at North Rim with a blazing display of color.

1.

2.

1. The majestic grandeur of the North Rim.

2. North Rim.

The fury of a storm breaks over the South Rim.

Powell Plateau in all its awesome
splendor.

1. Day breaks over Hopi Point.

2. Hopi Point at sunrise.

1.

2.

1. *The magnificent South Rim.*

2. *A dizzying view from Moran Point.*

3. *Trail View Point.*

Storm clouds gather over the South Rim.

Yaki Point.

1. *A breathtaking scene from Desert Point.*

2. *South Rim is warmed by the rising sun.*

1.

2.

GRAND TETON NATIONAL PARK

Wyoming

The Sweater Girl Mountains

THERE IS A STORY that one of the airlines whose routes span the Grand Teton range, in northwestern Wyoming, used to translate the name for curious passengers—understandably awed by the great pyramidal formations thrusting boldly up out of the prairies below—as the "Sweater Girl" mountains. In the original French, of course, spoken by the Canadian fur trappers who used to attend the mountain-man rendezvous at fur buyer David Jackson's "hole" in the early 1800s, *grand tetons* meant something considerably less demure. The name stuck, however, and in the intervening century and a half it has taken on some of the proud grandeur of the mountains themselves.

Seven peaks of the Tetons rise to more than 12,000 feet. Grand Teton is fully 13,770 feet. Impressive, but in Colorado there are 50 or more that are 2,000 feet taller; the Swiss Alps and the Himalayas reach considerably higher too. Yet the sheer, thrilling verticality of the Tetons makes them some of the world's most magnificent mountains. Classic block-fault formations, they seem to explode directly from the prairie on the eastern side, with no intermediary foothills to soften the visual blow.

Fairly recently, at least geologically speaking, massive but regionalized tectonic forces split the earth's crust at Grand Teton into a series of faults. The largest of these was the Teton Fault; the prairie side of this fracture sank, as if on a hinge somewhere to the east. That depression became the Jackson Hole (as it is now known) valley. On the west side, the country rock rose, pivoting upwards steeply and sharply. There is evidence that the combined displacement may have reached more than 25,000 feet before slumping, glaciation and erosion took their toll. The block that tilted up was at the time a more or less solid escarpment—a towering, 40-mile-long, north-south wall of ancient sedimentary stone—before fracturing, weathering and running water began to carve the formation into individual peaks separated only by precipitous ravines. The great glacier that expanded southward into the United States from Canada and the Arctic left its footprint on the Tetons too, in the form of trough-shaped valleys and hanging cirques. Although several thousand vertical feet have been worn or scraped off these mountains by now (the great ice sheets were completely gone only some 9,900 years ago) and the rock within them is among the oldest in North America, the still knife-like ridges, jagged horns and dizzying cliffs testify to the relative youth of the Teton Range. No worn-down Appalachians these. Tectonic activity is still going on, and earthquakes occasionally shiver through the Teton region. Hardly surprising; Yellowstone Park—the most active geothermal zone on earth, where the earth's crust is only about one-seventh its normal thickness and the planet's molten core comes very near the surface—lies immediately to the north of the Teton massif.

The large lakes—Jackson, Jenny, Leigh and others—along the foot of the scarp lie in some of the deepest crevices of the Teton Fault. Their boundaries are the moraines, or ridges, of coarse stone and gravel that were bulldozed up by the Ice Age glacier.

GRAND TETON National Park was established in 1929 at about 150 square miles, which took in the mountains and the most beautiful of the large lakes. A rancher named Pierce Cunningham had led the move to preserve the area "for the education and enjoyment of the Nation as a whole," and one of his line shacks is now preserved within the park as a testimonial to his foresight. In 1950 the park grew substantially, to its present 500 square miles, when the northern end of the Jackson Hole valley, which had earlier been designated a national monument, was added to the park. Local conservationists and, most notably, the Rockefeller family donated many acres of this land to the Park Service.

Despite the harsh winters, Jackson Hole itself has been inhabited more or less continually since about 10,000 B.C. The first white man to see it was most likely John Colter of Virginia, a member of the Lewis & Clark cross-country expedition who left the main group and veered north a ways alone during the winter of 1807-1808. With the mountains as landmarks, the "hole" served as a natural crossroads for Plains Indians as well as for the white fur trappers who began to spread through the Rockies in the 1820s; anthropologists believe that no one tribe claimed the Teton valley, but that Gros Ventre, Blackfeet, Shoshone and Crow bands all used it as neutral territory in the summer hunting seasons. The demand back East for beaver pelts tapered off sharply in the 1840s, and whites began to settle permanently in Jackson Hole in the 1880s.

Game is still plentiful today—moose, bison, mule deer, pronghorn antelope on the prairie and bighorn sheep in the mountains, and especially elk. (The great columns of antlers in Jackson's town square are made of antlers shed by the thousands of elk that come down from the high country annually to winter in the National Elk Refuge along Flat Creek.) There are predators too, of course: coyotes and black bears, and occasionally a grizzly foraging down from Yellowstone.

Today the park begins about five miles north of the information center outside the town of Jackson on Route 191, at the Jackson National Fish Hatchery. The mountains are the spine of the park, but the thread that ties it together is the Snake River. It starts up near the south boundary of Yellowstone Park and flows into the very top of Jackson Lake. It emerges from the lake again at Willow Flats, where there is a dam, and flows for 27 miles southward through the park. The dam, which enlarged Jackson Lake, was built early in the 1900s to provide irrigation water for ranchers over in Idaho, but today it plays an important role in flood control.

On a calm August day, the Snake meanders peacefully in its braided channels, where otters play and bald eagles compete with the ospreys for whitefish and native Snake River cutthroat trout. The water is always cold because of runoff from the glaciers and snowfields in the mountains above, but river runners, wildlife watchers, fishermen and birders always fall in love with this clean, blue-green waterway through the wilderness. During the spring melt or after a storm, however, the Snake changes its character completely. Then the abrupt wall of the mountains feeds runoff directly into the river, and it boils over its banks and races across the floodplain. Those high riverbanks of cobbles and gravel that seem to be unusually long, straight moraines are in fact dikes and levees built by the Corps of Engineers to try to keep the Snake more or less in its appointed path. Appearances to the contrary, the river is anything but "natural"; the many registered professional fishing guides and rafting companies here rely heavily on the largess of the Army for the "cfs"—the cubic feet per second of water released from the dam—they need to do business.

Teton Park has a broad array of visitor facilities, including a richly stocked Indian Arts Museum at the Colter Bay Center, and activities such as walks, hikes, campfire programs and slide lectures that are led by rangers. There are about 200 miles of trails that reach virtually all the park's remote valleys and lakes. Those who have the equipment and the experience to traverse them in winter often find exceptional vistas.

1. The Gros Ventre area of Grand Teton National Forest.

2. Trees color the dreary landscape of the Gros Ventre area of Grand Teton National Forest.

1.

2.

The flow of the Snake River wides its way through the Grand Tetons.

1. *Clouds converge over the Gros Ventre area of the Grand Teton National Forest.*

2. *The majesty of the Grand Tetons.*

1.

2.

1.

1. *A butterfly alights upon the wildflowers to doze in the afternoon sun.*

2. *The natural beauty of Grand Teton National Park shines in the late afternoon light.*

The setting sun colors Jenny Lake with a purple haze.

2.

A picturesque view of Oxbow Bend Turnout.

String Lake.

A powerful elk poses for a picture.

1. *Sunshine brightens this otherwise dreary view of the Gros Ventre area of Grand Teton National Forest.*

2. *Grand Teton National Forest.*

1.

2.

1. Mountains provide the back-drop for this field of greenery.

2. Cunningham Historic Site.

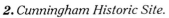

2.

GREAT BASIN NATIONAL PARK

Nevada

Wonders Above and Below Ground

IN 1986 THE WHEELER PEAK Scenic Area and Lehman Caves National Monument, in eastern Nevada, were combined—along with some other real estate from the Humboldt National Forest—to form America's newest national park. The "Great Basin" of the name is a regional depression—studded with impressive mountain ranges nevertheless—left behind when the mile-thick glacier of the most recent Ice Age melted away 10,000 years ago; it takes in virtually the entire northern half of Nevada from the Rocky Mountains eastward into Utah. The name Lehman comes from an Abe Lehman, who found the cavern in the 1870s; and Capt. George Wheeler, of the U.S. Army Engineers, who explored much of the Colorado Plateau region in the same time period.

As many national parks, Great Basin encompasses within its 77,000 acres several different terrains and ecologies, from sagebrushy Sonoran Desert to sub-Arctic/Alpine tundra, but with an added, underground dimension—a great limestone cavern second only to the enormous Carlsbad system.

The cave is on the eastern slope of 13,000-foot Wheeler Peak (which is the top of the Snake Range and the highest mountain in the Great Basin) in the piñon pine and juniper belt. The Park Service has installed a paved walkway about two-thirds of a mile long, complete with stairways, to view the cavern's many rooms. The constant 50-degree chill is something of a shock on a day when the surrounding desert may be twice that temperature. In the cavern there are terraced pools separated by delicate traceries of dams, great fluted columns and unusual shield-shaped formations called tom-toms that ring like a drum when struck, as well as many draperies, stalagmites and stalagtites. These "icicles" are formed by the steady accretion of minerals deposited by drops of water raining down from the cavern ceiling; as a measure of the vast blocks of time such a cave represents, consider that speleologists estimate stalagmites grow at a rate of about 1 inch in 750 years . . . .

Though this is essentially an arid zone, heavy winter snows and the high elevations mean that the peaks are white-capped for six months of the year, and runoff can be significant. There are, in addition, several year-round, spring-fed streams, notably Snake Creek and Lehman and Baker Creeks, which flow down out of canyons formed by the ancient glacier on either side of Wheeler Peak. There is also a Baker Lake, and alpine lakes named Johnson and Stella. The Great Basin is home to the full spectrum of western wildlife, from mountain lions and mule deer to rattlesnakes, kangaroo rats, golden eagles and herds of cattle.

Detail of Baker Creek.

Wheeler Peak.

1.

1. A wildflower bursts forth and clings tenaciously to life among the rocks.

2. Variable weather conditions wear away these rock formations, causing bits and pieces to break off and roll down the mountain.

An ancient Bristlecone pine tree grows among the rocks.

2.

Lichen covered rock formations near Wheeler Peak Road.

1. Detail of lichen covered rock.

2. Extraordinary rock formations near Wheeler Peak Road are reason enough for a double-take.

3. Verdant land provides a striking scenic view from Wheeler Peak Road.

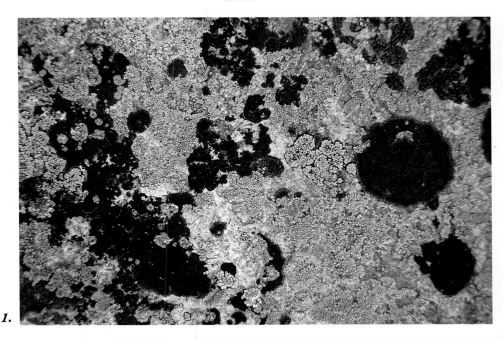

1.

2.

3.

1.

2.

3.

1. *Detail of the bark of a Bristle-cone pine tree.*

2. *The gnarled bark of a Bristle-cone pine tree.*

3. *One of the pine cones growing on a Bristlecone pine tree.*

This ancient Bristlecone pine is part of the history of Great Basin National Park, where some of the trees in this section are over 4,500 years old.

A wide variety of unusual rock formations can be explored at Lehman Caves.

GUADALUPE MOUNTAINS NATIONAL PARK

Texas

The American West Preserved

THERE IS AN 'EL CAPITAN' in Guadalupe Mountains National Park too, and it is as majestic a stair-step to the sky as El Capitan in Yosemite. But here, in the far western corner of Texas, abutting the New Mexico line, this relatively new park is itself part of the renowned Capitan Reef. A quarter of a billion years ago, a 400-mile-long, semicircular reef began to form in the teeming tropical sea that covered this part of the Southwest. Over empty eons of time, the sea dried up, the reef was buried in great drifts of sediments and then began a period of uplift and the erosion that always accompanies such mountain-building. The Guadalupe Range is an exposed part of that reef, and its cliffs are thick with the fossils of ancient marine animals and plants.

The mother lode for research geologists is McKittrick Canyon, in the northeast corner of the park. An oil-patch geologist named Wallace Pratt began buying land there around 1920. His goal was to safeguard the complex natural riches of the canyon, where to date more than 500 different fossils have been identified—and along with them has come valuable information about earth's past. In 1959 Pratt donated his 5,000-plus acres to the federal government. Shortly afterward, the Hunter family, which had amassed 72,000 acres nearby, also offered its holdings for a park, at the bargain price of about $21 per acre.

Guadalupe Peak, the highest mountain in Texas, stands 8,700 feet above sea level and about 5,000 feet above its surroundings. Half a dozen others nearly match it, and the entire massif rises—stony-bare, gray and ochre and pink in the ever-changing light—from the semi-arid plains of the Chihuahuan Desert. Up in the core of the high country lies a spectacular bowl, a 2-mile-wide pocket densely thicketed with conifers—ponderosa pines, aspen, Douglas fir and white pine.

Mountain lions, black bear, wild turkeys, mule deer and many other animals live in the Guadalupe Highlands, but the most remarkable are the 70 or so elk, the only wild herd of them in Texas. Originally native, the present elk are the descendants of a core stock transplanted here in the 1920s from Wyoming and South Dakota.

The desert at the foot of the mountains is a completely different ecosystem, with agave and prickly pear cactus, yucca, junipers and other shrubs providing shelter for the abundant coyotes, lizards, snakes, scorpions and insects. To hike the trail up McKittrick Canyon, along its spring-fed creek and through the scrub oaks, is to walk from one environment into the other, and the transition is equally interesting. In 1966 the Guadalupe Mountains were set aside in perpetuity as a national park.

The last rays of the setting sun can be seen over El Capitan.

The west side of El Capitan viewed from the road to Williams Ranch.

1. *El Capitan.*

2. *The splendor of El Capitan and the Guadaloupe Mountains is enhanced by the sunset.*

1.

2.

1. *Engelmann Pricklypear cactus.*

2. *Apache Plume.*

3. *Engelmann Pricklypear cactus and Apache Plume grow wild at the base of the Guadaloupe Mountains.*

3.

McKittrick Canyon.

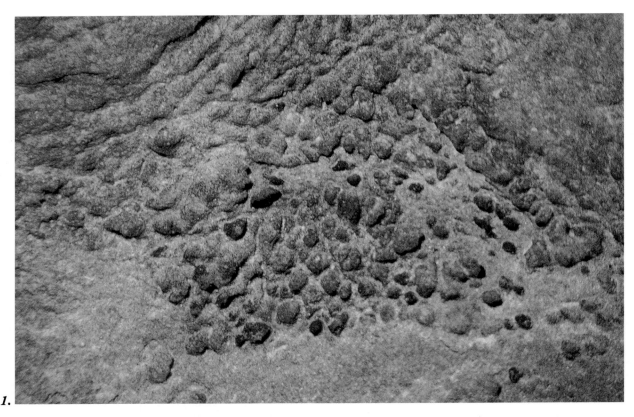

1. *Fossilized sponge.*

2. *The cool, clear creek water of McKittrick Canyon eddies around the rocks.*

View from the Nature Loop Trail.

1.

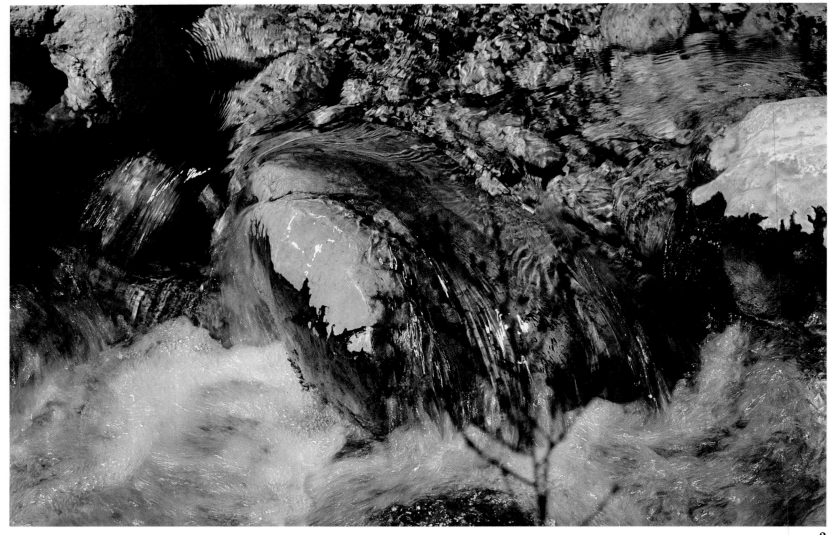

2.

1.

2.

1. This cactus is better known as the Walking Stick Cholla.

2. The rugged beauty of the Guadaloupe Mountains.

3. Manzanita Spring is a freshwater spring located near the historic Frijole Ranch.

3.

LASSEN VOLCANIC NATIONAL PARK
California

The Sleeping Giant

NORTHEASTERN CALIFORNIA, where the Sierra Nevada range meets the Cascades extending down from Oregon, is as geologically unstable as any portion of the circum-Pacific "Ring of Fire." That is what geologists call the edge of the Pacific Plate, one of the more mobile vast sections of the earth's crust that are eternally shifting relative to one another—growing at mid-oceanic ridges, colliding with each other, forcing one edge up over, or down beneath, another. Some of the most earthquake-prone parts of the world—Japan, the Aleutian Islands, the coast of California—are affected by the Pacific Plate. And, as its name indicates, the Ring of Fire sees more than earthquakes alone; it is also a belt of active, and extremely destructive, volcanism; caused, of course, by the same tectonic movement.

Like all the peaks of the Cascades, Lassen, the southernmost, is a volcano. In fact, until Mount St. Helens in Washington exploded so devastatingly in 1980, Lassen Peak had the distinction of being the most recent volcanic eruption in the Lower 48 states. (Alaska and Hawaii both have perennially active Pacific-Plate volcanos themselves. There were eruptions nearby as recently as 1851, but Lassen itself had lain dormant for some 400 years. That changed on May 30, 1914, when, with an impressive discharge of steam, Lassen entered a seven-year period of intermittent eruptions. In the first year alone, the peak erupted more than 150 times. The climax came in May of 1915, when rivers of hot lava poured down the mountain's flanks, bringing huge boulders and mud slides with them. Then a blast of steam and ash shot skyward as high as seven miles; airborne particles fell as far away as Nevada, and ash and rock slides cut a mile-wide swath of destruction through five miles of forest on Lassen's northeast side.

National attention focused on the mountain, and in 1916 it was declared a national park. President Teddy Roosevelt, impressed by its significance as a volcanic "laboratory," had already set the area aside as a national monument in 1907. Besides Lassen Peak, the park also contains another, much smaller volcano called the Cinder Cone, and extensive lava beds, fumaroles, hot springs and boiling mudholes. Towering Lassen Peak, geologists have determined, is but a "plug dome" that had grown on the site of a much larger volcano—Mount Tehama—that exists only as a caldera today.

Since 1921 Lassen Peak has slumbered peacefully. But it is no more likely to stay that way than the San Andreas Fault, a few hundred miles west and south, is to stop moving. Some scientists feel that Lassen and neighboring Mount Shasta are now the most likely of the Cascades to join St. Helens on the active list.

Bumpass Hill, the scene of volcanic activity, where lava flowed along its course of destruction for many years.

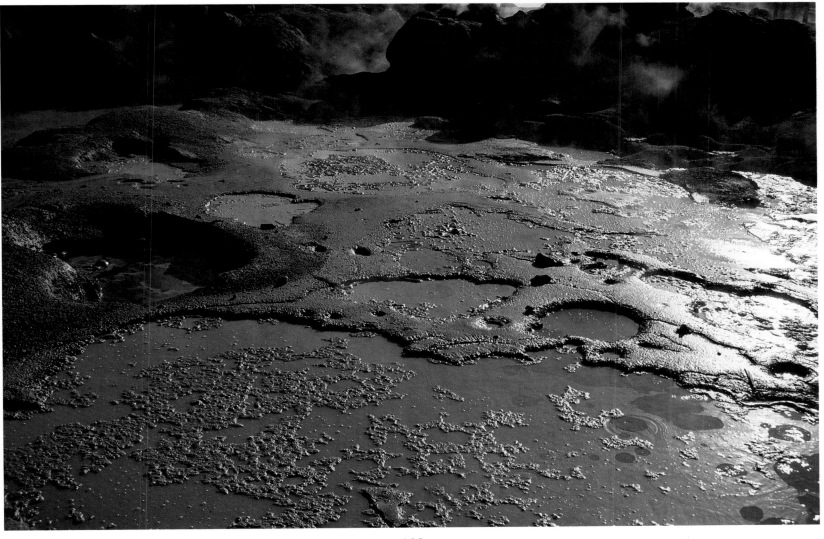

Water forcefully washes over the rocks that lay in its path.

Detail of Kings Creek Falls.

1. *A purple sea of wildflowers mark the trail to Bumpass Hell.*

2. *Bumpass Hell.*

3. *The trunk of a fallen tree is an ideal location for grass to grow anew.*

MESA VERDE NATIONAL PARK
Colorado

World of the Ancient Ones

A STONE AGE CITY is Mesa Verde, the only national park set aside to preserve the works of man instead of nature. Its villages were the homes of a mysterious culture that flourished here a millennium ago and then vanished. We don't even know what these people called themselves, but the Navajos who came after them gave them the name *Anasazi*, the Ancient Ones.

The Anasazi people lived at Mesa Verde for more than 700 years. The ruins document the evolution of a culture. It began about 600 A.D. when, under some unknown impetus, the nomadic hunter-gatherer bands of this region gradually coalesced and put down roots at Mesa Verde. The Anasazi became farmers who relied on basic irrigation techniques. Their staple crops were beans, maize and squash. Their first fixed dwellings, on the mesa top, were pit houses, half above and half below grade, with timbers at the corners to support roofs of juniper boughs and dried mud. The people became expert basket makers and potters, and invented the bow and arrow and the atlatl, or spear thrower. They learned to make and use stone axes, stone-tipped digging sticks for plowing and planting and specialized tools for fire-making, cooking, weaving, sewing and leather work. A highly structured social order developed as well.

Within two centuries they had moved into the type of block-and-mortar dwellings now called pueblos. The pit house wasn't abandoned, however; it evolved into the underground kiva (which means ceremonial room). Kivas were roughly analogous to churches, and were probably used for social and religious functions. In about the years 1000 to 1200 their architecture blossomed. With carved sandstone blocks and mud mortar, they built single-, double- and triple-story multi-family complexes with as many as 50 rooms. Many of these survive in the park today, especially those built in the last century of Anasazi civilization when, for unknown reasons, the people moved off the mesa top into the openings in the cliffs.

This is one of many mysteries surrounding the Anasazi—why they "went underground." Around the end of the 13th century, on the heels of what some investigators say was a 20-year drought, the Ancient Ones left Mesa Verde (and their other villages) and, over the next few generations, let themselves be assimilated into other tribes, the forebears of today's Navajos and Hopis. Their departure was sudden enough to prevent them from completing the great Sun Temple, atop the mesa. In 1906 the Congress passed the Antiquities Act, to protect historic objects on federal lands. In that same year and in that same idealism, Mesa Verde was declared a national park.

Cliff Palace.

Square Tower House ruins at sunset.

A section of Cliff Palace.

Detail of Spruce Tree House.

Spruce Tree House.

Square Tower House is ablaze with color from the setting sun.

1. *Fire Temple.*

2. *Oak Tree House.*

1.

2.

1. *A camouflaged deer is easy to miss among the trees and underbrush of Mesa Verde National Park.*

2. *The sun sets, painting a brilliant display of color in the evening sky.*

MOUNT RAINIER NATIONAL PARK

Washington

Mountain of Memories

THE WORLD has many higher mountains, but perhaps none are more majestic and memorable—and simply beautiful—than Mount Rainier, the white-capped monarch of the Pacific Northwest's Cascade Range. From ground level the mountain seems to fill the sky. Even from six miles up in an airliner, en route to Vancouver or Anchorage, to see Rainier shouldering upward massively into the atmosphere, is to be impressed all over again. At 14,400 feet, the summit stands almost 8,000 feet taller than any of the lesser peaks nearby. In Seattle and Tacoma, 60 miles to the north, and all the other communities around Puget Sound, Rainier is simply "the mountain," a seemingly eternal presence. At ground level, it can be picked off the horizon from more than 100 miles away.

That is, in fair weather. The peak stands tall enough to break completely through the layer of moist Pacific air flowing west-to-east in the atmosphere, and the result is heavy precipitation year-round and weather patterns that are occasionally chaotic—if only in the middle of the mountain. While thick, swirling clouds cloak the entire massif from the view of people on the ground, the upper third of the peak is often completely above the clouds and basking in that startlingly clear sunshine known only to airline passengers. Snow falls all over the mountain, but between 5,000 and 10,000 feet, at the level of Paradise Park, Rainier develops a belt of snow that is often 30 feet deep or more every winter. In the winter of 1971-72, some 93 feet of snow fell here—a world record at the time. It's common for the three-story Paradise Inn—on the south slope of Rainier—to be buried beyond its roof in snow.

This annual snowpack is an important contributor to the Rainier ecosystem, which depends upon its water content, and to the character of the mountain itself. For although Rainier is a dormant volcano, born out of the fantastic fire of the earth's molten magma, on the outside it is shrouded the year around in permanent ice. Glaciers exist where snow falls in greater quantities than can melt at any time during the full seasonal cycle; over time the snow deepens and compacts into ice; gravity eventually tugs the ice formation downslope, and nature's bulldozer goes to work. There are 27 glaciers, big enough to have names, ringing Mount Rainier's summit. They grind slowly down to oblivion in the warm lower elevations while each winter's snowfall feeds them from above. Together the ice fields comprise almost 35 square miles, making Rainier the largest single-mountain glacial system in the Lower 48.

Ice climbers and winter mountaineers flock to the mountain for its own challenges and to train for expeditions in Alaska, the Himalayas and the Andes. Consequently, the rangers who manage the park have had to become specialists in winter search-and-rescue work, for every year ill-prepared—or simply unlucky—people get lost, snowed in or injured on Rainier's demanding terrain. In spring and summer, avalanches are a particular hazard, as warmer weather loosens the thick blanket of snows, especially in the steep couloirs of bare rock, where there are no trees to anchor the surface. Summers, when conditions are better (but still marginal, for severe weather can boil up any time), thousands of people manage to reach the summit of Rainier every year, with the help of professional guides. In decent weather, it is a two-day trip.

The first recorded successful ascent of Mount Rainier happened to be a two-day trip too, but that was a stroke of luck. The peak was "conquered"—if such a term can ever be applied to it—on August 17, 1870, by two nature-loving men named Hazard Stevens and Philemon Beecher Van Trump. A Yakima Indian named Sluiskin had guided them through the forest and up onto the mountain, which in the native language was called Takhoma. Despite his formidable warnings against Takhoma's bitter and changeable weather, they decided to try to finish the climb. When they failed to return to camp that night, Sluiskin gave them up for dead; no one could survive a night up there. That they did, and were able to walk back down the next day with the peak in their pockets, was entirely due to the fact that they'd found an area of rock warmed by volcanic steam vents in which to spend the night. Several years earlier, upon his first sight of Rainier, Van Trump had recorded in his journal a passionate desire to reach the top; in 1888, he had the profound satisfaction of himself guiding the great naturalist John Muir, founder of the Sierra Club, to the summit. Muir's enthusiasm helped crystallize public sentiment for the great mountain, and the national park was established in 1899, from what had been designated the Mount Rainier Forest Reserve. Today the park takes in more than 235,000 acres, or almost 400 square miles.

THE VAST, mile-thick glacial sheet that spread down from Canada during the last Ice Age—which ended only some 10,000 years ago—extended far to the south of Washington state. It flowed around Mount Rainier and left its upper story exposed. The cold inaugurated severe ice conditions on the mountain as well, of which the present-day glaciers are only a remnant. The slopes of the Rainier volcano (and of the entire Cascade Range, a string of volcanos that is part of the circum-Pacific Ring of Fire) took on their dramatic shape then, when ice gouged out the ridges and valleys that contribute to its majesty. Someday, when erosion has reduced it to a worn nubbin of rock, Rainier may be only a humble shadow of its present-day self. Then again, the mountain may abruptly vanish in an almighty roar—as did its neighbor, Mount St. Helens. Or a more peaceful eruption may simply "grow" Rainier a few feet higher someday, to counter the effects of erosion. As a volcano, Mount Rainier is anything but extinct; the steam that sometimes comes from the vents and craters on top attest to that.

Rainier's sheer bulk, and the symmetry and noble proportions of its crown, would almost be enough; but the beauty of the landscape below the ice—the subalpine meadows with their carpets of wildflowers, and then the lush, green surrounding lowland lakes and forests also elevate the mountain into a class all its own. In this region where such distinct climatologic zones meet there is abundant wildlife, from the trout in the clean waters to mule deer and marmots in the foothills and then the mountain goats of the high country.

While much of the precious old-growth forest of the Pacific Northwest is being shortsightedly razed to feed foreign hunger for timber, the Rainier ecosystem, at least, is safe. In the not-too-distant future, unless state and federal legislators come to their senses, we may have to visit Mount Rainier and the other northwestern parks in order to remember what this majestic forest looked like—Douglas fir, red cedars, sitka spruce, and western hemlocks that stand sometimes 200 feet tall above the ferns and mosses of the understory. Only the great groves of giant redwoods are more hushed and cathedral-like. For generations of visitors Rainier has meant lasting memories.

A breathtaking view of an Alpine meadow with Mr. Rainier in the background.

Deer frolick about the slopes of Mt. Rainier.

Mt. Rainier is covered by a blanket of snow.

Mt. Rainier is mirrored in Reflection Lake.

The early morning sun bathes Mt. Rainier with its warmth and light.

1.

1. *Flowers grow wild along the edge of Reflection Lake.*

2. *Wildflowers bloom in the warmth of the sun.*

2.

NORTH CASCADES NATIONAL PARK

Washington

America's Switzerland

THE CASCADE MOUNTAINS of Oregon and Washington extend northward into British Columbia and south down into northeastern California. They include Lassen Peak, Mount Rainier, Shasta, Mount St. Helens—household words, almost all. Now, do you know Boston Peak or Sahale Peak? How about Mount Shuksan or Magic Mountain? Mount Logan? Eldorado? Baker? Few Americans outside Washington state do. These are the premier peaks of that nearly impenetrable section called the North Cascades, which abuts the Canadian border. Sometimes they are called the American Alps, for they have the same jagged, upthrusting, lean and hungry look to them, and from certain vantage points they march away to the horizon as if gentle lands were no more. Storms and rain from the Pacific are trapped in these mountains; much of the year they stand draped in snow, and even highway access is limited. Ice fields are permanent fixtures here—the park contains more than half the glaciers in the Lower 48. Great lakes and rushing rivers cleave their valleys.

The less adventurous can taste the wild splendor of the North Cascades from the comfort of their automobiles, or from the deck of the *Lady of The Lake*, the passenger ferry that plies Lake Chelan. But to experience the mountains means to get in among them. And there are plenty of them—more than 1,000 square miles of wilderness has been permanently set aside here, for recreational use or to be preserved as wild parkland. And there are many more miles of buffer zone around them. North Cascades National Park is divided into two sections, the North Unit and the South Unit, that are separated by a 3-mile-wide strip called the Ross Lake Recreation Area. This forms a corridor for the trans-montane North Cascades Highway and also contains all three of Seattle City Light's hydroelectric generating stations. Below the South Unit lies Lake Chelan National Recreation Area. Its headquarters, a wilderness town called Stehekin, can only be reached by foot, boat or floatplane. And completely encircling all these protected zones are four national forests plus two officially designated wildernesses and—across the border—Canada's Manning Provincial Park.

The ensuing decades of destruction to the woods and waters of the Cascades galvanized public attention, and in 1968 Congress was moved to take this region out of the national forest system and to protect it as a national park—"to preserve for the benefit, use, and inspiration of present and future generations certain majestic mountain scenery, snow fields, glaciers, alpine meadows and other unique natural features in the North Cascade Mountains."

A spectacular view of Ross Lake dazzles the eye and eases the mind.

Detail of Ladder Creek Falls and moss covered rocks.

Wahkeena Falls.

OLYMPIC NATIONAL PARK

Washington

Land of Endless Exploration

THE OLYMPIC PENINSULA is the northwesternmost tip of the continental United States—a vast corner of the state of Washington that is bounded by the Pacific Ocean on the west and on the north by the Juan De Fuca Strait, the broad channel that separates the United States from Vancouver Island, British Columbia. The peninsula is one of those storied regions of America, much like Michigan's Upper Peninsula or Maine's Aroostook County, that are separate from the mainstream because of an accident of geography and so have been able to cling to another time. No multilane freeways connect this peninsula to the busy cities of Puget Sound, less than 50 miles to the east; its forests, coastline and wildlife also belong to another time. The peninsula is a jewel, the heart of which is Olympic National Park, one of the least visited of all the major parks.

It is an enormous chunk of real estate—almost a million acres; just over 1,500 square miles (significantly larger than Rhode Island). But in effect it is even larger, for the park is in two pieces that between them capture, and seem to include, the Olympic National Forest. Most of the park lies in the mountainous interior of the peninsula, but there is a separate, narrow, 57-mile-long strip of park that hugs the Pacific shore and takes in nearly all the offshore reefs and islands. In truth, Olympic National Park is three parks together: a high alpine wilderness; a zone of deep, heavily forested valleys; and a craggy, wild coastline.

The peninsula was largely unexplored by whites until 1885, although a Portuguese seafarer named Juan de Fuca reputedly came ashore in 1592, and British, American and Spanish voyagers alternately laid claim to the region from 1774 until the Canadian-American border was established in 1818. Several expeditions late in the 19th century brought back to Washington the news that this was a rare and wonderful place, and in 1897 President Grover Cleveland created the Olympic Forest Reserve. Teddy Roosevelt further protected a portion of it by setting it aside as a national monument in 1909, and then in 1938 President Franklin Roosevelt signed the national park into law. The narrow coastal strip was added in 1953 and expanded to its present size only in 1976.

The single most dominant force in the park (and on the peninsula itself) is the Pacific Ocean. Here, at about 48° North Latitude, the sea comes crashing ashore with the full force of weather systems generated in the Gulf of Alaska, the Bering Sea and the vast reaches of the entire North Pacific. Air temperatures are moderate but chilly year-round, and fierce storms and gales of lashing rain are common. The tidefall is significant, and the surf and inshore currents are often irresistibly strong. Together, these elements have carved out a coastline that may be the most dramatic (and the most un-spoiled) in the Lower 48 with steep headlands eroded—no, water-blasted—into fantas-tic shapes; a littoral zone that teems with life; and an ever-changing collection of flot-sam and jetsam thrown onto the beach that ranges from Japanese net floats to the trunks of huge trees. Despite their size, these blown-down trees have been stripped of their bark and branches in the rough surf and finally cast ashore with negligent ease by the sea.

This is a beachcomber's paradise. Hikers pick their way over the giant logs and along the rocks with the crash of the waves and the call of seabirds in their ears. Gulls, ospreys, eagles and oyster catchers hunt overhead. Raccoons and river otters pick over the plentiful shellfish. Harbor seals crawl ashore to sun themselves on the rocks, and seasonally the gray whales show themselves beyond the surf, on their annual migration between the Sea of Cortez and Alaskan waters. In the forests behind the beach live black bear and deer.

The Pacific affects the inland portions of the park too, by sending ashore on the pre-vailing winds the moisture that makes this perhaps the wettest region of the United States. Usually, 150 to 200 inches of rain fall here annually, and fog sometimes settles in for what seems to be weeks. Together with the relatively mild temperatures, these unusual conditions have produced an even more unusual phenomenon: one of the few temperate-zone—as opposed to tropical—rain forests on earth. (The others are on New Zealand's South Island and in southern Chile.) Along the coastal plain and in the shel-tered, westward-facing valleys of the Hoh, Queets, Quinalt and Bogachiel rivers the trees grow so thickly that in places falling snow simply never reaches the ground. This zone is a botanist's delight, a fantastically complex ecosystem where more than a thou-sand species of plants grow. The dominant trees are the western hemlock, the sitka spruce and the Douglas fir, and record examples of each are found here—there are firs more than 300 feet tall and 20-plus feet in circumference; they are perhaps a thousand years old. They share space with red alder, big leaf maples, western red cedars, black cottonwood and others, each festooned with living draperies of fungi, vine maples, ferns, mosses and lichens. Everything is green, luxuriant, dripping with water and bursting with life. A rain forest does not need fire to clear its understory and return the nutrients in its deadfalls to the soil; the mild temperatures and high humidity ensure that rapid decay does it instead. Spruce and hemlock seedlings, among others, unable to find room on the verdant forest floor, usually begin to grow in the rotting wood of fallen "nursery" trees.

A VITAL LINK in the rain forest ecosystem is the rare Roosevelt elk (named for Teddy, the conservationist president). Olympic Park was created in part as a preserve for these shy woodland elk, which are larger and more social than the wapiti of the Rocky Moun-tains. Today their numbers have increased and stabilized, and they form the largest unmanaged elk herd in the United States. Although visitors to the forest often see elk sign—tracks, pellets, browsed shrubs—they rarely catch more than a glimpse of the animals themselves, a far cry from the elk-posing that goes on in Yellowstone and Grand Teton parks.

Moving inland from the rain forest, the land begins to climb. Annual average temper-atures slowly drop. When the red cedar is gone, the so-called montane forest has taken over. Moving higher again brings on the subalpine zone, where the growing season is shorter and more of the precipitation falls as snow. Clearly, this is no rain forest; and higher still, the trees thin out completely and give way to broad alpine meadows that are dotted with small glacial lakes and, at least in early summer, carpeted with flowers. The elk and deer move into this high country as the weather warms, joining the moun-tain goats and Olympic marmots.

Here, where the environment has changed so radically, only the heavy snowfall pro-vides a clue to the nearness and influence of the ocean. In stark contrast to the warm and verdant lowlands, the bare and stony upper reaches of 8,000-foot Mount Olympus, the roof of the park, are clothed in glaciers. There are a dozen or so smaller ice- and snowfields even farther east, but so little moisture gets past the Olympic peaks that, not many miles farther on, in the rain shadow, semi-arid conditions prevail.

Waves crash into the rocks at Ruby Beach.

1.

2.

1. *Ruby Beach is alive with the colors of the setting sun.*

2. *The surf beats against the shores of Ruby Beach.*

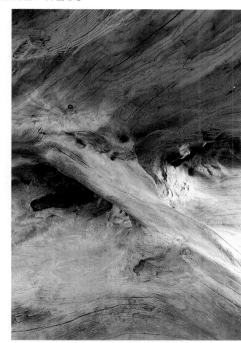

1. Detail of tide pool with sea anemones.

2. Detail of a driftwood log.

3. Starfish hide in the undergrowth at the edge of the water.

4. Sea anemones living in a tide pool.

Marymere Falls.

1. *Wildflowers fill the countryside with their beauty.*

2. *Wildflowers blowing in the breeze at Olymic National Park.*

3. *Driftwood is plentiful on the shore of Rialto Beach.*

1.

2.

3.

Captivating view of the sunset from the top of Hurricane Hill.

1.

1. *A peaceful winter scene is viewed from Hurricane Hill.*

2. *A nursing log rests on the floor of a rain forest.*

One of the magnificent views along the Hurrican Hill Trail.

2.

A grazing mountain goat eyes the camera.

PETRIFIED FOREST
NATIONAL PARK
Arizona

The Rock-Candy Land

A UNIQUE NATIONAL PARK must have unique problems, and the Petrified Forest does. Everywhere, every ancient formation of stone is disappearing, by way of erosion and weathering; here, these chunks of stone are vanishing just as quickly—but into the pockets of visitors. And in the years after the site was discovered, in the 1850s, and before the park was created (that was in 1962, and part of the area had already been set aside as a national monument since 1906) gem collectors and jewelers were removing pieces of petrified wood by the barrow-load, and commercial operators were doing it with dynamite and trucks and the Santa Fe Railroad, which laid track through what is now the park in 1883. Public outrage in the Arizona Territory was finally awakened when a company built a mill to crush the logs into abrasive powder for industrial use. Fortunately, it never went into production.

What sparks all this acquisitiveness? The great logs of semi-precious stone—onyx, jasper, amethyst, carnelian, opal and agate—lying about on the ground. Literally logs, for within the park rest six "forests" of now-horizontal trees; thousands of them, some more than 150 feet long, that over the ages have been metamorphosed. More than 200 million years ago, this region was a great, flat flood plain cut and braided by watercourses. The trees, it is thought, came from higher country nearby and were stranded here in the aftermath of periodic floods. Before oxygenation could set them to rotting, lesser flows covered the trees up with mud, sand and silica-rich volcanic ash. Then the alchemy began. Groundwater percolated into the trees and slowly began to replace the wood tissue with silica, the hard oxide of silicon that makes, among other things, glass and quartz. The bright swirls of color within the "wood" are stains of other minerals such as iron and manganese.

The remarkable trees sometimes obscure the rest of the park, which contains some of the most interesting human and fossil records of the American Southwest. Newspaper Rock, for example, near the Puerco Indian Ruin, is a huge stone monolith liberally covered with Indian petroglyphs that probably date back almost 2,000 years. It is only one of some 300 native sites. The north end of the park is a large section of the Painted Desert, a fantasyland of mineralogy that seems to reflect every possible earth tone from green through the spectrum to red, plus hues of white and yellow. And the Petrified Forest has been a destination spot for so long that one of its modern buildings, the Painted Desert Inn, built at Kachina Point in the 1920s, has itself been listed as a National Historic Landmark.

1.

2.

1. *The grounds are covered with petrified logs in all shapes and sizes at the Petrified Forest National Park.*

Detail of the surface of a petrified log.

2. *Inside view of petrified logs.*

Petrified logs in the process of forming litter the land.

Detail of the cross section of a petrified log.

REDWOOD
NATIONAL PARK
California

THE THICK, MOISTURE-laden air of the northern Pacific Ocean, moving ever eastward over the United States and Canada, does more than simply drop hundreds of inches of snow every winter in the Cascade Range, or nurture the rain forest of the Olympic Peninsula. Right along the California coast, in a temperate, foggy zone that extends from just below San Francisco up into southern Oregon, it creates the sort of climatic conditions that redwood forests flourish in.

When the Spanish padres were moving into California from Mexico to establish their missions, there may have been 2 million acres of these mighty trees here. What has happened since then has been—or should be—a graphic lesson in the effects of wide-scale timber cutting. By the millions, the trees were razed and milled and fashioned into long-lasting railroad ties, shingles, beams, picnic tables, patio decks, gazebos and outdoor furniture.

The damage takes two forms. First is the simple destruction of the tallest living things on earth—organisms that, when mature, stand 200 to 300 feet tall and average about 600 years of age. The tallest of all trees is a redwood in the park's Tall Trees Grove, along Redwood Creek. In 1963 it was found to be a few inches over 367 feet; it's probably more than a thousand years old. Of course, the cut-over areas can be replanted, and in mere centuries we'll be able to marvel at these stately creatures again—stand humbled at their roots and crane our necks upward to the vast, cathedral-like canopy above.

The second form of logging damage is done to the land where the trees are erased. In most cases, between the cutting itself and the collateral injury of the skidder trails and haul roads, the ground is left denuded, crushed, exposed to runoff and erosion. This removes the vital topsoil and sends it downslope, often into nearby streams or rivers. The regenerative capacity of the land is diminished; the habitat of hundreds of animal species is destroyed; and siltation and runoff threatens the ecosystem of the waterways.

Citizen's groups have been formed since the very early 1900s to try to protect California's redwood stands. Until 1968, the timber industry was able to circumvent their efforts with ease. But in that year, Redwood National Park was created. It was only a thin, 58,000-acre strip along the coast, but it was a beginning. Cutting continued on adjacent private lands, so 10 years later Congress added another 48,000 acres and then established a Park Protection Zone of another 30,000 acres in the Redwood Creek watershed, upstream of the park. This too is hands-off to timbering.

Giant redwood trees keep the forest in shadows at the Jedediah Smith Redwoods State Park.

A giant redwood tree amazes the observer with its immense size and beauty.

Gazing up at the treetops has a dizzying effect at the Jedediah Smith Redwoods State Park.

The top of a redwood tree in the
Lady Bird Johnson Grove.

1.

2.

1. *Plant life clogs the water in Lagoon Creek.*

Waves gently wash the coast at Enderts Beach.

2. *Seagulls doze in the midday sun at False Klamath Cove.*

1. *Picture-perfect wildflowers grow in abundance.*

2. *A butterfly takes time to stop and smell the flowers.*

3. *A Roosevelt Elk strolls in the warm light of the setting sun.*

2.

1.

3.

ROCKY MOUNTAIN NATIONAL PARK

Colorado

The Roof of America

THE SCULPTED NORTHERN portions of the great Rocky Mountain cordillera, up in Alberta, may be the most impressive to look at. The southern sections, that rise from New Mexico's desert, might be the most colorful. But here in northern Colorado's Rocky Mountain Park, they scrape the sky. One-third of the 50 tallest peaks of the Rockies are in this 400-square-mile pocket; more than 100 of the park's summits reach 11,000 feet or more. And fully a third of the entire park lies above the timber line.

Many lakes, most of glacial origin but a few that have been dammed up by beavers, dot the park. Groves of green quaking aspen mix in with the darker, denser stands of lodgepole pine, Engelmann and blue spruce. Broad expanses of alpine meadow, sometimes brilliant with blue columbine and other short-lived wild blooms, hug the lower shoulders of the mountains. Higher still lies the sub-Arctic tundra, a brittle zone of fragile lichens, mosses and tiny stemmed plants that can withstand their harsh environment far better than they can tolerate the footsteps of hikers. Bare rock canyons, enormous scree slopes and glaciated clefts yawn between the peaks.

It is tempting to think that this is the great wilderness that the early fur trappers and mountain men knew, but of course it is not. The West has been just as brutalized—if less obviously—by the 19th and 20th centuries as the East. Hereabouts, while elk, mule deer, black bear, bighorn sheep, coyotes and other species thrive, the grizzly bear, the wolf, the buffalo and perhaps the mountain lion have been gone for decades. So have the Indian bands. Ranchers, sheepherders and prospectors have all left their mark and trails galore.

The Colorado Gold Rush brought thousands of settlers here in 1859, but the first white man "of record" was Maj. Stephen Long, U.S. Army, who led an exploration party through these parts in 1820. At that time the Rockies, part of the Louisiana Purchase, had only been American territory for 17 years. Longs Peak, at 14,225 feet the highest of all of Colorado's mountains, is named for him. John C. Fremont, one of the intrepid handful of explorers of the West that also includes John Wesley Powell and Lt. Zebulon Pike, came here in search of an easy pass through the Continental Divide to the Pacific. They opened the door; it was a dedicated conservationist named Enos Mills who made sure it didn't swing too far. In 1886, at 16 years of age, he built a cabin in the valley of Longs Peak, and the grandeur of the mountains came to dominate his life. His campaign to preserve this corner of the territory came to fruition in 1915, when "his" Rocky Mountain National Park was created. He was there at the ceremonies.

Ominous storm clouds gather in the sky over the rugged terrain.

1.

2.

1. A storm threatens to intrude on this peaceful sunset.

2. Dramatic sunset viewed from the top of the Alpine Visitor Center Trail.

Plant life flourishes at Nymph Lake.

Swiftly running Ouzel Falls creates the illusion of a mantle of white.

1. *A Pika sits at attention, ready to flee at a moment's notice.*

2. *Reverie is definitely encouraged at Dream Lake.*

Peace and quiet descend over Bear Lake with the setting sun.

Bear Lake prepares for the coming night.

1. Sunsets over the Rockies are as magnificent as the mountains themselves.

2. Relics from the past await tourists from the present on the Never Summer Ranch.

1.

2.

1. *Close-up of an old, gnarled tree along the Crater Trail.*

2. *A fawn listens intently for the sounds of approaching danger.*

3. *A desolate view along the Crater Trail.*

1.

2.

3.

*One of the majestic views along
the Crater Trail.*

1.

2.

1. Experience a soothing view along the Bowen/Baker Trail.

2. Jagged rock formations can be seen from the Old Fall River Road.

The Colorado River flows near the Never Summer Ranch.

Extraordinary view near Gore Range overlook.

1. The scent of vibrant wildflowers wafts through the air.

2. View from the old Fall River Road.

1. *Fellfield Rocks.*

2. *Wildflowers thrive among the rocks.*

3. *Unusual rock formations ease the barren scene.*

1.

2.

3.

SEQUOIA/ KINGS CANYON NATIONAL PARKS
California

The 'Range of Light'

THESE ARE TWO adjoining parks that together stretch 65 miles, south to north, and as much as 35 miles east to west. The "kings" of the name might well refer to both the trees *and* the lofty summits of the Sierra Nevadas; the former are the largest of all trees, and the peaks, some of which top 14,000 feet, include Mount Whitney, the very highest in the Lower 48.

But Kings Canyon got its name from the early Spanish, who called the river that carved it the *Rio de los Santos Reyes*, the River of the Holy Kings. If they thought that divine intercession helped form the canyon, it's understandable—along its winding nine miles, the walls rise as much as 8,000 feet above the water. In dispassionate terms, it is a hydro engineer's dream, and the Kings River narrowly avoided being dammed for power generation. This is California, after all, with the nearly insatiable needs of the largest population among the states. Fortunately, California boasts the largest and most vocal conservationist groups as well—which leads to the reasons for these parks.

There are two because they were created some 50 years apart. They are separated only by an imaginary line, and are today managed by one administration. But the two names emphasize that these are two entities established to save two different natural wonders—the mountain wonderland and the river, and the trees. Kings Canyon, the northern park, was established in 1940. It contains some of the grandest mountain-and-lake landscapes in North America. Sequoia, signed into existence in 1890, has the distinction of being the second oldest national park in America—five days older than its neighbor, Yosemite, also a small victory for conservationists.

There are less than 100 groves of giant sequoias left, all on the west slope of the California Sierras. They are remnants of the ancient forests that, like New Zealand's podocarp trees, stood on earth when dinosaurs lived.

The California sequoias are all that survived the Ice Age that ended 10,000 years ago, and they have barely survived us. Because of their thick, water-saturated bark, they are virtually impervious to fire; their metabolisms are so geared to extreme longevity that there is no clear, complete life cycle, no apparent reason that a healthy sequoia should ever die. The so-called Giant Forest, in the northwest corner of Sequoia Park, is the home of the General Sherman Tree—more than 272 feet tall and estimated to be nearly 4,000 years old. It was named by James Wolverton, the trapper who discovered the tree in 1879 and who had served under, and admired, Sherman. Close by stand generals Grant and Lee, only slightly shorter, but still as tall as 25-story skyscrapers.

Moro Rock proves to be an ideal vantage point from which to watch this rainy sunset.

Glimpses of the clear, blue sky can be seen through this forest of giant trees.

1. *Grizzly Falls.*

2. *Roaring River Falls in Kings Canyon National Park meets its destiny at the waiting pool.*

3. *A drizzily sunset hides the beauty of this view from Moro Rock.*

1.

2.

3.

A blazing sunset colors Sequoia National Park with brilliant yellows, reds, oranges and golds.

The strength of this mighty Sequoia can be seen in its massive trunk.

Breathtaking views such as this can be seen in the Cedar Grove section of Kings Canyon.

YELLOWSTONE NATIONAL PARK

Wyoming-Idaho-Montana

Where the 18th and 20th Centuries Meet

YELLOWSTONE in all its primal splendor has always been the most famous of America's national parks and the home of some of the country's best-loved natural symbols, from Old Faithful to Fishing Bridge to the late Smokey the Bear. Its 2 million acres carry large numbers of bison, elk, moose, antelope, mule deer and other animals, many of whom seem to like to grandstand spectacularly along the park's roads. Over those roads cruise the great herds of Winnebagos and Airstreams and poptop trailers, bearing the American tourist; Yellowstone, whose spooky volcanic fumaroles and bubbling hot mud pools and spewing geysers worried the Indians, is always a must-see on the visitor's migratory route. Yellowstone, America's premier natural attraction, the world's largest geothermal zone, was in fact the very first national park, the one that sparked hundreds of others around the world. And Yellowstone is also famous for the many controversies that have swirled around its management. The central issue, which amounts to an attempt to define "modern wilderness," is itself still fuming today.

Yellowstone Park was legislated into existence in 1872. George Catlin, the naturalist and Indian painter of the early 19th century, may have overstated the case when he suggested that all of America west of the Mississippi be set aside as the "nation's park." But in the late 1800s there was an undeniable groundswell of (ill-informed) public admiration for wilderness—or at least the notions of wilderness that were being romanticized by public figures ranging from Buffalo Bill to Henry Thoreau. Perception and reality began to collide in Yellowstone country shortly after the park was born. The Native American was part of the glamorized concept that led to the preservation of wilderness, but far from including the "noble savage" in the park, the federal government promptly moved a band of Sheepeater Indians out and onto a reservation.

Today fact and fiction are still at loggerheads, this time over the question of re-establishing timber wolves in Yellowstone. The last resident wolf was shot in 1926, the local culmination of a long government campaign to eradicate predators in the American West. Now biologists say the park ecosystem is incomplete without them, and that wolves—along with the present coyotes and black and grizzly bears—must be present to balance the food chain. Neighboring ranchers, who expect the wolves to forage as readily on their sheep and cattle as on the park's hoofed denizens, have a hard time grasping this turnaround. There have been other reversals, equally controversial, concerning the grizzly bear, sportfishing and even hunting in the park.

Unlike Waterton/Glacier Park, at the other end of Montana, Yellowstone is accessible enough to receive millions of visitors annually. Yet, unlike Yosemite Park, Yellowstone is still remote enough to be genuinely wild. It is also blessed with an astonishing diversity of habitat; like an American Serengeti, there are more animals here than anywhere else in the Lower 48. These animals and urban man meet head-on in Yellowstone; it is the prime interface between this century and two centuries ago. (In August 1986, my wife and I were driving through the Hayden Valley. On the far bank of the Yellowstone River, where it veers close to the road, lounged a grizzly—eating a bison. Within minutes, hundreds of cars clogged the road, and alert rangers with walkie-talkies were circulating through the crowd, making sure griz and man stayed on their sides of the river. Within one of the park-service vans undoubtedly waited a well-armed "bear team" just in case.) Friction is inevitable—maybe even welcome, for it is here in the Yellowstone laboratory that some of America's most intelligent wildlife, fisheries, and environmental policies have finally been worked out.

THE PARK is impressive at any season, even when its 300 miles of scenic loop roads are bearing the brunt of midsummer traffic. For those who forsake the asphalt and set off with rucksack, camera, binoculars and map (back country permits are required for overnight hiking), there are more than a thousand miles of trails. In many cases it takes only a few minutes of walking to crest a ridge and gaze upon a landscape that has remained intact since 1872. Save for the occasional sight of a jet airliner, the view could date from centuries even before that, for there are no more cavalry platoons or Indian tribal bands on the move here.

Manmade features are inevitable, of course, in such a well-traveled public place. Some—Mammoth Hot Springs (which was once Fort Yellowstone, U.S. Army), Lake Village, Grant Village, Old Faithful and Canyon—are almost towns, with restaurants, motels, campgrounds, post offices, garages and even a hospital, in addition to the expected visitor centers and exhibits. A few of the buildings, such as the Old Faithful Inn, are among the most remarkable in the western United States, and have taken on a historical lustre themselves.

At the height of its season, with its staff of hundreds of people in place, the entire park has the air of a colony, a place disconnected from everyday reality but still busy. In winter, when the roads become ski and snowmobile trails, and bison wallow through snowdrifts, and the thermal springs make hotspots of fish and insect activity in the midst of icy streams, the park feels more like an enormous work of art.

THE NATIONAL OUTCRY over the great Yellowstone fires of the summer of 1988 has abated, but the public confusion has not. After hearing again and again from all parties concerned, most Americans still cannot make an informed decision over whether natural fires in wilderness areas should be fought, or even whether wildfires are a benefit or a disaster. Although many people around the world saw news film of smoke and flames seemingly ringing Old Faithful, and some very public portions of the park were blackened, only a small fraction of Yellowstone's acreage burned. Very few animals died. No streams were fatally silted in during the following spring, even where runoff passed over ash beds and banks bare of vegetation. And ground cover began to restore itself within weeks after the fires went out.

The flames, in fact, released an abundance of nutrients that had been locked up in thousands of tons of dead and downed timber that were lying inert on the ground, the accumulation of more than a century with *no* fires. Yellowstone's forests received a vital dose of ash fertilizer, which is now nourishing plant and animal life alike, helping keep disease and insect infestations at bay and generally strengthening the entire ecosystem. In places where mature stands of trees disappeared, sunlight could again reach the ground and, together with the dose of nutrients, spur new growth and natural productivity. The "sterilized" sections of the park are seeing a post-fire bloom.

A forest is a living thing that changes as it proceeds from birth to maturity. Fire allows the process to begin again. Far from being destroyed, Yellowstone is merely different, and probably better for it. The fires, and the intense research and debate they spurred, have been called an ecological event without precedence. Merely another chapter in Yellowstone's long, sometimes turbulent, often honorable history.

1.

1. A bison herd roam the snow filled Lamar Valley.

2. Cutoff Mountain stands tall in this beautiful winter scene.

2.

A rainbow shines through the mist at the Grand Canyon in Yellowstone National Park.

1. A vast expanse of wilderness is part of Yellowstone National Park.

2. All the colors of the rainbow can be seen at the base of Lower Falls.

*A brilliant sun brings out the in-
credible colors of Artist Point.*

Tower Falls takes the plunge at 132 feet.

A misty sunrise paints an eerie picture of the Yelowstone River.

1.

1. Hot water action on volcanic rock created the palette of colors in the Grand Canyon at Yellowstone National Park.

2. Bison hungrily search for food in the winter snow.

Calcite Springs overlook.

2.

Porcelain Basin is the hottest exposed area in Yellowstone National Park.

1.

2.

1. Smoke from Porcelain Basin's intense heat drifts skyward.

2. Roaring Mountain.

Canary Spring is located in the Mammoth Hot Springs section of Yellowstone National Park.

Daily deposits of travertine (calcium carbonate) form the terraces at Mammoth Hot Springs.

1. *The spectacular terraces of Minerva Spring are located at Mammoth Hot Springs.*

2. *A buffalo feeds in the early morning hours as mist rises from the Yellowstone River.*

3. *Minerva Spring.*

Grand Prismatic Spring is the largest hot spring in Yellowstone National Park.

1.

1. An elk wading in the water regards the camera with a questioning stare.

2. Detail of Midway Geyser Basin.

2.

Mist slowly rises over Grand Prismatic Spring.

The sun reflects sharply in the Morning Glory Pool.

1. Beauty Pool sparkles with brilliant blues and greens.

2. Beauty Pool.

1.

2.

1. *The green of Abyss Pool shines through at West Thumb Geyser Basin.*

2. *Close up of Abyss Pool.*

3. *Steam from Steamboat Geyser fills the air.*

1.

2.

3.

Old Faithful, Yellowstone's most famous geyser, spouts high into the air.

1.

2.

3.

1. Castle Geyser.

2. Echinus Geyser.

3. The fragile crust forms interesting patterns in West Thumb Geyser Basin.

1. A marmot stares down his visitors.

2. Drops of water glisten as sunlight hits the erupting Grott Geyser.

1.

2.

1.

2.

1. *A brown bear smells the air for any scent of approaching danger.*

1. *A statuesque elk stands his ground.*

2. *It's playtime for two frolicking bear cubs.*

2. *A moose walks through the forest in search of his herd.*

1.

2.

1. *Raging fires burned out-of-control throughout Yellowstone National Park during the summer of 1988.*

2. *Dense smoke from fires at Yellowstone National Park filled the sky.*

3. *Intense heat, flames and smoke threatened the park and its wildlife.*

1.

2.

3.

1. *Not long after the fires burned out, regrowth occurred slowly but surely.*

2. *The devastating results of a fire mar the countryside on the road between Canyon & Norris.*

1. *This sign of rebirth in the aftermath of the fire is an encouraging and welcome sight.*

2. *A roaming bear enjoys the sights at Yellowstone National Park.*

1.

2.

YOSEMITE NATIONAL PARK
California

Shaped by Glaciers and Man

SOME 150 MILES from San Francisco, in eastern California, a surreal granite valley extends like a natural highway into the western slope of the central Sierra Nevada range. The valley floor, though almost unnaturally flat, is carpeted with wildflowers, subalpine meadows, oak groves and stands of mixed conifers. The sheer walls of this unique landscape, which are about a mile apart, shoot perpendicularly upwards for 2,000 to 3,000 feet and sometimes more. Mule deer graze in the lush grass and dizzying cascades of water hang like smoke against the cliffs. Visitors have likened it to a roofless cathedral.

This is the Yosemite Valley of the Merced River, and around it lies the 761,000 acres, or 1,200 square miles, of Yosemite National Park. The land is alternately serene and spectacular, always majestic. But since Civil War times, the park has been under siege by visitors. Today, with millions of urbanites only hours away by car and camper, its roads, tramways, hotels, campgrounds and bridle paths are sometimes choked and Yosemite is pressured as never before. But it is surviving and prospering, and its managers have drawn up a plan that should protect it as never before.

The first whites to report having seen the valley were the officers and men of California's Mariposa Battalion, who in 1851 cautiously rode in while tracking the Indians that had been attacking gold-mining settlements. The Indians were the Yosemite band of the Miwok tribe; "Yosemite" was their clan totem, the grizzly bear. There were, in fact, about two dozen native villages in the valley at the time—unlike Yellowstone with its hellish volcanic features, this region impressed everyone with its livability.

Had the Indians seen it 10,000 years before, when an immense glacier lay hundreds of feet thick over the Merced River and was bulldozing flat the sides of the great granite domes, they would have been otherwise impressed. Today's awe-inspiring scenery is the product of ages of earthquakes, volcanism, glaciers and the erosive effects of countless avalanches and spectacular storms.

Attracted by tales of the valley's rugged scenery, visitors began to arrive from coastal California within the decade. In 1864, Congress made a special grant of 48 square miles of the valley and environs to the state as a park, and then in 1890 established Yosemite National Park around the state park. Inevitably, conflicts arose over management, and in 1906 California ceded its part to federal control. Then, until the National Park Service was formed 10 years later, the U.S. Army ruled Yosemite. Pioneering conservationist John Muir explored the region and wrote many of his journals here. Artists and scientists have followed his lead ever since—poets, painters, naturalists and photographers such as the late Ansel Adams.

LOOK CLOSELY at the badge of a National Park Service ranger. The symbol on it is the seed cone of a Yosemite giant sequoia, the trees that were one of the reasons for creating the park. There are sequoias (related to the giant redwoods; Sequoya was the tribal name of George Guess, the American Indian scholar who created the written alphabet of the Cherokee language) elsewhere along the Pacific coast, but Yosemite has three famous stands of the trees. Chief among them is the Mariposa Grove, at the southern tip of the park about 35 miles below Yosemite Village, which holds some 200 sequoias. Two of these trees have tunnels cut through them, and were made famous in postcards and newsreels in the days when it was still seen as a moral imperative for man to leave his mark upon the wilderness. The two other groves—Tuolumne and Merced—lie on either side of the Merced River near Crane Flat, on the eastern boundary of the park.

Alongside the geological grandeur of the Yosemite Valley, the sequoias stand proudly. Though they are the largest living things on earth, and among the oldest—the tree known as the Grizzly Giant, in Mariposa, is estimated to be 2,700 years old—their rich colors and stately shapes may be even more impressive than their sheer size. Sequoia wood and bark are fire-resistant, and scars on some healthy trees indicate they have survived forest fires in the past. The Park Service's now-obsolete no-burn policy actually worked against these trees, which, as do some other conifers, need fire to propagate. Their seeds need mineral soil and sunlight, neither of which are found in mature stands of sequoias, where the understory has usually been filled with fir and cedar. Fire clears new seedbeds and opens the forest floor to light, and today the Park Service takes over for nature in a careful program of prescribed burns in the groves to keep the overall population healthy. Young sequoia trees are now more abundant than they have been for decades. Cars aren't allowed beyond the parking lot near Mariposa, but in summers a tramway runs through the grove, and the hiking trails are open year-round. Skiers and snowshoers who brave the winter find a hushed and tranquil forest.

Yosemite was the cradle of the Sierra Club, and the site of some of America's earliest conservation/preservation battles. One of the bitterest swirled around a proposal to dam the Tuolumne River canyon in the park—as spectacular perhaps as the Yosemite Valley itself—for water for San Francisco. It did happen, in 1913, forming the Hetch Hetchy Reservoir.

Animals are not a severe problem in Yosemite; to date there have been no bear fatalities. People create Yosemite's problems. Rafters can turn miles of the Merced into a watery version of any southern-California freeway. Climbers and hang-gliders dot the cliffs of El Capitan and Half Dome and Glacier Point. John Muir said, "Walk away quietly in any direction and taste the freedom of the mountaineer"—but too many inexperienced "recreationists" mean many man-hours of search-and-rescue work for the park's experienced ranger and volunteer teams. They have to deal with everything from illegal parachuting off the cliffs (some jumpers die) to simple hypothermia. And crowds bring with them the potential for trouble. Park rangers have had to become police officers expert in combatting drugs and thievery, speeding and drunk and disorderly behavior. There is even a 16-person jail in the park, and a federal magistrate's court. On national park land, any offense, even littering, is a federal crime.

But the park today is in better shape than a decade ago, and a decade hence should see even greater progress. The general management plan is to set aside more than 1,000 square miles—the park's back country—as protected wilderness, forever free from development. The 770 miles of trails that span it will stay, but some of the posh, privately operated tent camps will be phased out. The park plans also to move many concessions and even Park Service facilities outside its borders, and to replace many of the cabins and motels with campgrounds, and those open only to advance registration. Tour buses, such as the shuttles that now cover the eastern half of the valley, are another step towards the eventual goal of eliminating private vehicles altogether. "Scenic" overflights from nearby cities have been curtailed too, as sources of noise and visual pollution for those on the ground in the park.

Yosemite's physical features have been protected for years. Now the intangibles will be considered too, to safeguard the aesthetic quality of the experience.

A rainbow at sunset over Half Dome heightens the beauty of the scene that is visible from Glacier Point.

1.

2.

1. Rainbow over Half Dome.

2. A rainbow sparkles in the waters of Emerald Pool.

1. New fallen snow covers Yosemite Valley in a mantle of white.

2. Yosemite Valley—a winter wonderland of snow.

1.

2.

1. Vernal Falls.

2. The sheer rock face wall of El Capitan stands tall in the sun.

3. The warmth of the sun melts the winter snows in Yosemite Valley.

*Vernal Falls swiftly tumbles to the
pool below.*

Winter in Yosemite Valley as seen from Tunnel View.

1. *Clouds lazily drift across the sky over Mount Dana.*

2. *Reflection in Mirror Lake.*

3. *A formidable view of Half Dome from Mirror Lake.*

1.

2.

3.

1.

1. Yosemite Valley swelters in the summer heat.

2. A captivating sunset is seen from the Tunnel View.

Tunnel View.

2.

1. *Majestic Mount Gibbs provides the background for this wilderness scene.*

2. *Olmsted Point is captured by the colorful hues of the setting sun.*

ZION
NATIONAL PARK
Utah

The 'City of God'

THE SITE OF SOLOMON'S temple, in Jerusalem, was called Zion; and Zion came to mean the abode of God. Even a brief drive through this national park will show the visitor the appropriateness of the name. From nearby Salt Lake City, the early Mormon settlers, who verged on religious zealotry, saw no blasphemy in it—in fact it was they who dubbed this "Land of Rainbow Canyons" Zion, and used it as a retreat.

The broad strokes of nature in the park are sheer-walled Zion Canyon, created by the North Fork of the Virgin River, and the Kolob finger canyons, smaller clefts gouged out by the forks of North Creek, in the northwestern corner. And in between lies country no less spectacular—a petrified forest, natural stone arches and tunnels, a swamp in the midst of desert, vivid "hanging gardens" clinging to the cliffs and irrigated by wavering waterfalls and some of the most brilliantly colored sandstone in the entire red-rock region. Zion is part of the "Great Circle" of national monuments, parks and recreation areas of the Colorado Plateau that makes the American Southwest one of the most scenic regions on the continent; in location and in the variety of its terrains and seasons, Zion might be regarded as the centerpiece. Its majestic towers and canyons were formed by the same 250-million-year cycle of deposition, uplift, faulting, erosion and weathering that sculpted all of southern Utah.

The first whites—Spanish soldiers and missionaries—passed through this land when Americans were winning their freedom from England, and Zion was the home of Paiute Indians. Then, after the colonial wars, Americans turned their attentions westward. Capt. John Fremont explored the Colorado Plateau in the 1840s, and the Mormon wagon trains who followed relied upon his notes to bring them to the Great Salt Lake. Fur trappers and mountain men came south out of the Rockies.

The narrows of Zion Canyon are a vertical slash into the earth. The walls are 2,000 to 3,000 feet high, pages on which geologists can read 13 million years of stratigraphy and continental upheaval. The non-scientific pilgrim, however, can find as much to be awed about. Hiking the Narrows means miles of wading the Virgin River at the feet of these awesome cliffs. Along some stretches they close to within 20 feet of each other, and at the bottom all you can hear is the water against your legs, the beating of your heart and the echo of all that time stretching away up to the sunlight. It doesn't seem possible that such a gentle creek could have cut this incredible ravine, but when weather threatens, the Park Service closes the canyon. Flash floods roar through here with the sound and force of monster freight trains. Mere stone doesn't stand a chance.

1.

2.

1. *Sunrise at Zion National Park.*

2. *Kolob Canyon.*

Unusual rock shapes along the Zion-Mt. Carmel Highway can be attributed to erosion.

Rock shapes create odd patterns of cracks and grooves along the Zion-Mt. Carmel Highway.

1. *Massive cliff walls are the most striking attractions in the park.*

2. *Rocks, colored in white and orange, form interesting strata.*

3. *Sunlight captures the extraordinary rock formations at Zion National Park.*

1.

2.

3.

1. Steep cliff walls border the Zion Canyon Scenic Drive.

2. The size of trees in proportion to this rock formation boggles the mind.

1.

2.

1. *A peaceful view along the Kolob Canyons Road.*

2. *The hard, stony face of these rock formations create a dismal picture.*

1.

2.

1.

1. *The drive along the Zion-Mt. Carmel Highway is filled with beautiful sights.*

2. *Spectacular canyons can be viewed along the Kolob Canyons Road.*

2.

NATIONAL MONUMENTS AND RECREATION AREAS

'In wildness is the preservation of the world'

WHEN HENRY DAVID THOREAU wrote those words late in the 19th century, he was thinking of Walden Pond, which today is surrounded—just beyond its encircling ring of trees—by Boston's endless suburbia; the pond even has a bathhouse and a beach. True wilderness is many miles away. But Walden Pond still has the ability to calm the soul. Its water is still blue-black in the shade. The oaks around it still drop their acorns. Fish and small animals (perhaps even a few whitetail deer) live there more or less as they always have. The visitors who walk the shore daily in the warmer months usually don't spell out just why they've come—"We are here to see a part of life that is older than we are, and larger than we are"—but they understand it. The real world is preserved within those scant acres.

As far back as the 1890s, unspoiled lands have been set aside in America to preserve them from logging, mining, grazing and flooding under dams. Conscious decisions were made by enlightened people to save the high watersheds and stands of forest "for the public good." There may have been some disagreement as to exactly what that meant; certain early preservationists probably regarded those forests and waters as long-term national bank accounts, held against the day when they too would have to be pressed into service. Lands of spectacular natural features or enduring historical significance became national parks or monuments; millions of acres of timberlands became national forests. Today the parks and monuments are essentially safe from all but being loved to death. America's national forests, however, which exist under a different mandate, are increasingly the front lines between conservationists and resource companies.

National recreation areas are another category altogether—outdoor playgrounds dedicated to boating, swimming, hunting, fishing and even off-road driving, often at the expense of wilderness. But they have their place too. The water skiers who roar over Lake Mead may not be inclined to hike the miles of nearby high country and desert that are also part of that recreation area, but they are drawn to the lake in part by the undeveloped country that surrounds it. For decades, the solution to ever-increasing tourist traffic in Yosemite or Yellowstone or Acadia was to build another Visitor Center, open another trail, pave another road, let more raft companies or concessionaires or muleskinners in, and then publish a bigger brochure. The erosion of wilderness was gradual, by inches over years, and genuinely unintentional, but none the less real and deadly.

A canyon crevice at Antelope Canyon in Arizona.

1. Antelope Canyon in Arizona is home to these spectacular rock formations.

2. Lake Powell is located in Arizona at the Glen Canyon National Recreation Area.

3. Lake Powell.

1.

2.

1. A highlight at Death Valley National Monument in California is Zabriskie Point.

2. Badwater at Death Valley National Monument in California is known as the lowest point in the Western Hemisphere.

1. The floor of Death Valley National Monument in California is covered with parched, dry earth.

2. A field of wildflowers swaying gently in the summer breeze at Death Valley National Monument in California.

1.

2.

Winter snow blankets White Sands National Monument in New Mexico.

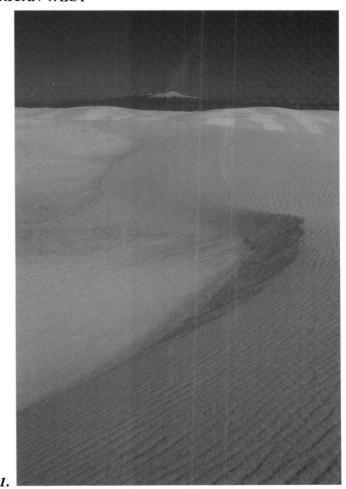

1. A desolate scene from White Sands National Monument in New Mexico.

2. With a little imagination these unusual rock formations at the Joshua Tree National Monument in California can remind visitors of almost anything, even prehistoric dinosaurs!

The Joshua Tree National Monument in California.

1.

2.

1.

2.

1. *Dinosaur fossils imbedded in a rock wall at Dinosaur National Monument in Utah/Colorado.*

2. *Indian petroglyphs can be seen at Dinosaur National Monument in Utah/Colorado.*

The Green River winds its way through Dinosaur National Monument in Utah/Colorado.

A captivating view from the Oregon Dunes National Recreation Area in Oregon.

1. *North view of Cedar Breaks National Monument in Utah.*

2. *Cedar Breaks National Monument in Utah.*

1.

2.

MOUNT RUSHMORE NATIONAL MEMORIAL

South Dakota

Democracy's Monument

ONE OF THE MOST unusual, not to say the oddest, of America's national public lands is this fantastic sculpture of four great statesmen gazing imperturbably out over South Dakota from the rim of Mount Rushmore. Totalitarian political systems are being swept away around the globe, to be replaced with American-style liberties. This heroic sculpture, a symbolic summary of the political thought that carried America through her first 150 years, has renewed worldwide meaning.

George Washington, on the far left, led the struggle for independence and was there at the birth of the Republic. Thomas Jefferson, the philosopher president, put into words the inchoate yearnings for personal freedom and political self-determination. Abraham Lincoln, the emancipator, was able to bring a "house divided" together again, and he freed not only the black man but all men, for all time. And blunt-speaking Theodore Roosevelt brought an environmental outlook to the White House while overseeing America's emergence as a world power.

Doane Robinson first proposed the idea of a great sculpture in the Black Hills in 1923 and found artist Gutzon Borglum. It was Borglum who suggested the four presidents and Borglum who picked out Mount Rushmore, for its shape and size and for its close-grained granite that would hold the necessary detail. Both the state and federal governments gave their assent, and Mount Rushmore was declared a national memorial in the fall of 1925. Private donations came in, enough to get started in August 1927.

With dynamite, hammers and wedges, workmen began to rough out the cliff face to form Borglum's "canvas." While the broad contours were being shaped, Borglum prepared the models for the heads, eventually ending with figures one-twelfth the actual size. These were lifted up to the edge of the cliff, to guide the workers.

The federal government finally stepped in, contributing more than 80 percent of the 1 million dollars needed. It also took 14 years to reach the stage that the statues are at today, though the actual work occupied only six years and a few months. The final misfortune was that Borglum died in March 1941. His son, Lincoln, carried the job through its final six months. The first of the great heads, George Washington, was formally dedicated on Independence Day 1930. At just under 6,000 feet in elevation and 500 feet higher than the surrounding countryside, Mount Rushmore is far taller than the Great Pyramid at Giza, and the heads are the largest carved figures in the world. They are scaled to a human 465 feet tall.

On the side of Mount Rushmore in the Black Hills of South Dakota are carved the faces of Presidents George Washington, Thomas Jefferson, Abraham Lincoln and Theodore Roosevelt.

Mount Rushmore.

BADLANDS NATIONAL PARK

South Dakota

Prairie Memories

THE TERM 'BADLANDS' is about as accurate a description of this marvelous terrain as "barrens" is when applied to the treeless tundra of the Northwest Territories. Which is to say, not at all. Canada's arctic barrens teem with life; and South Dakota's Badlands National Park is a place of haunting beauty and otherworldly landscapes. There are moments, of course, when the visitor may be able to imagine the despair of a 19th-century hunter or rancher who got "turned around" in this moonscape, slowly realizing that he'd ridden past this particular oddly shaped stone tower three times already . . . .

The Badlands Wall stretches east and west across almost 100 miles of Dakota prairie. It is a wide, upthrust belt of soft sedimentary rock formations that are ceaselessly being sculpted by the freezing and thawing, the expansion and contraction, of rain water and snowmelt in their cracks and crevices. But this is not the bone-dry, dusty, red-rock country of southern Utah and New Mexico; this is the northern Great Plains, where between the peaks and monoliths and crazy-quilt stone hedges run swathes of wild grasses. The wolf is gone, but coyotes, elk, mule deer, bighorn sheep and antelope roam here. A herd of a few hundred bison now roam freely through Badlands National Park. This region was part of the bison's migratory pattern, and a century and a half ago perhaps 50 million of those great animals trod the Great Plains.

The principal reason that such astonishing numbers of animals were able to live here is the wild grasses of the prairie—hardy and nutritious plants that, nationwide, have become rare themselves. They can withstand the 100-degree summer droughts, the prairie fires and the ferocious, cow-killing blizzards of the northern plains. But there was one thing they could not withstand. The Winchester rifle didn't tame the West; the steel plow did. Few visitors to this park might think to look down from the buttes and the grand vistas to the grass underfoot, but it is a mixture of blue grama, buffalo grass, western wheatgrass, side-oats grama and other species that together bear little resemblance to a suburban lawn.

The fertility of the soil eventually attracted ranchers and farmers, but then it was the combined effects of the Great Depression and the Dust Bowl that helped reclaim this portion of the plains. In the decade after 1929, when the stock market collapsed, many settlers gave up fighting the weather and the economy and sold their lands back to the federal government. In 1939, under the urging of local senators, Franklin Delanore Roosevelt was able to coalesce these holdings into a Badlands National Monument.

1. *Mountain vista at Badlands National Park in South Dakota.*

2. *Majestic rock formations at Badlands National Park in South Dakota.*

1.

2.

1. Rock formations and canyons are common sights at Badlands National Park.

2. Snow covered rock formations await the spring thaw.

1.

2.

1. Nature at its best is a beautiful sight to behold.

2. Fossils imbedded in the rocks at Badlands National Park in South Dakota.

INDEX

Numbers in italics indicate pictures.

Abyss Pool, *236*
Acadia, 265
Adams, Ansel, 246
Alpine Visitor Center Trail, *190*
American Alps, 155
Anasazi, 10, 41, 51, 133
Andes, 146
Antelope Canyon, *266, 267*
Antiquities Act, 8, 133
Appalachians, 95
Arches National Park, 9, 10, *11-18,* 41
Artist Point, *218*
Badlands National Park, 283, *284-286*
Badlands Wall, 283
Badwater, *268*
Baker Creek, 107, *108*
Baker Lake, 107
Balance Rock, *16*
Battle of Shiloh, 84
Bear Lake, *194-196*
Beauty Pool, *235*
Big Bend National Park, 8, 19, 20, *21-30*
Big Spring Canyon, *49*
Biscayne Park, 8
Black Hills, 279, *280-281*
Boquillas Canyon, 19, *26, 27, 28*
Borglum, Gutzon, 279
Bowen/Baker Trail, *200*
Bowman Lake, *80*
Bright Angel Trail, 84
Bryce Canyon National Park, 31, *32-40*
Bryce, Ebenezer, 31
Buffalo Bill, 213
Bumpass Hill, *128-129, 132*
Calcite Springs, *223*
Canary Spring, *227*
Canyon & Norris, *243*
Canyonlands National Park, 41, *42-50*
Capitan Reef, 59, 117
Capitol Gorge, *55*
Capitol Reef National Park, 51, *52-58*
Carlsbad Caverns National Park, 59,
    60-62, 107
Castle Geyser, *238*
Castolon Peak, *23, 24, 30*
Catlin, George, 7, 213
Cedar Breaks National Monument, *278*
Cedar Grove, *212*
Chaco Canyon, 41
Chihuahuan Desert, 19, 117
Chisos Mountains, 19, 20, *22, 28*
Cinder Cone, 127
Civil War, 7, 8, 10, 84, 245
Cleveland, President Grover, 161
Cliff Palace, *134-135, 138*
Colorado Gold Rush, 187
Colorado Plateau, 8, 51, 84, 107, 257
Colorado River, 8, 10, 41, 83, 84, *201*
Colter, John, 96
Continental Divide, 72, 187
Crater Lake National Park, 63, *64-70*
Crater Trail, *198, 199*
Cunningham Historic Site, *106*
Cunningham, Pierce, 96
Cutoff Mountain, *215*
Davis, Ray, 59
Dead Horse Point State Park, *46*
Death Valley National Monument, *268, 269*
Delicate Arch, 10, *12-14, 18*
Department of the Interior, 7, 8, 59
Desert Point, *94*
Devil's Garden, 9

Devils Tower, 8
Dinosaur National Monument, *274, 275*
Dixie Land, 31
Dream Lake, *193*
Dust Bowl, 283
Echinus Geyser, *238*
Egyptian Temple, 51, *56*
El Capitan, 117, *118-121,* 246, *250*
Elephant Hill, *49*
Ellis Island, 8
Emerald Pool, *248*
Enderts Beach, *185*
Entrada Sandstone, 10
Fairyland Point, *38*
Fall River Road, *203*
False Klamath Cove, *184*
Fellfield Rocks, *204*
Fiery Furnace, *17*
Fire Temple, *143*
Fishing Bridge, 213
Fish and Wildlife Service, 8
Flathead, 72
Fletcher, Colin, 84
    The Man Who Walked Through Time,
    84
Forest Service, 8
Fremont, 51, *52*
Fremont, John C., 187, 257
Frijole Ranch, *126*
Fuca, Juan de, 161
Garden of Eden, *18*
Garden Wall, 71
Gates of the Arctic, 8
General Grant, (See Sequoia/Kings Canyon
National Parks)
General Lee, 205
General Sherman Tree, 205
Giant Forest, 205
Glacier Point, 246, *247*
Glen Canyon National Recreation Area, 8,
    267
Goat Mountains, *21*
Going-to-the-Sun Road, 72, *82*
Goosenecks, *58*
Gore Range overlook, *202*
Grand Canyon National Park, 8, 31, 41, 83,
    84, *85-94,* 216, *222*
Grand Prismatic Spring, *230-231, 233*
Grand Staircase, 31
Grand Teton National Park, 95, 96, *97-106,*
    162
Grandview Point, *47*
Grant Village, 214
Great Basin National Park, 107, *108-116*
Great Depression, 283
Great Northern Railway, 72
Great Pyramid at Giza, 279
Green River, *48,* 84, *275*
Grinnell, George, 71
Grinnell Glacier, 72
Grizzly Falls, *209*
Grizzly Giant, 246
Gros Ventre, *97, 99, 105*
Grott Geyser, *239*
Guadalupe Mountains National Park, 117,
    118-126
Guadalupe Peak, 117
Guess, George, 246
Half Dome, 246, *247, 248, 253*
Hayden Valley, 214
Hetchy, Hetch, 8, 246
Hidden Lake, *78*
Himalayas, 95, 146
Honeycomb Rock, *54, 55*

Hoodoos, 9, *35, 38*
Hopi Point, *89,* 133
Hot Springs, 7, *25*
Humboldt National Forest, 107
Hurricane Hill, *168-171*
Ice Age, 19, 83, 96, 107, 146, 205
Indian Arts Museum, 96
Inspiration Point, *36*
International Peace Park, 20
Island in the Sky, 41, *46, 48*
Jackson, David, 95
Jackson Hole, 95, 96
Jackson Lake, 96
Jackson National Fish Hatchery, 96
Jedediah Smith Redwoods State Park, *180,*
    182
Jefferson, Thomas, 279, *280-281*
Jenny Lake, 96, *101*
Johnson Lake, 107
Joshua Tree National Monument, *272, 273*
Kachina Point, 173
Kaibab National Forest, 31, 84
Kings Creek Falls, *131*
Kings River, 205
Kolob Canyon, 257, *258, 263, 264*
Ladder Creek Falls, *158*
Lady Bird Johnson Grove, *183*
Lagoon Creek, *184*
Lake Chelan National Recreation Area, 155
Lake MacDonald, *77*
Lake Mead Recreational Area, 83, 265
Lake Powell, *267*
Lake Village, 214
Lamar Valley, *215*
Land of Rainbow Canyons, 257
Landscape Arch, 10, *15*
La Sal Mountains, *18, 49*
Lassen Peak, 127, 155
Lassen Volcanic National Park, 127, *128-*
    132
Lehman Caves National Monument, 107,
    116
Lehman Creek, 107
Lewis & Clark, 96
Lincoln, Abraham, 279, *280-281*
Logan Pass, *73, 74,* 155
Long, Maj. Stephen, 187
Longs Peak, 187
Lost Mine Trail, *29*
Louisiana Purchase, 187
Lower Falls, *217*
Lower Two Medecine Lake, *82*
Lunch Creek, *74*
Mammoth Hot Springs, 214, *227-229*
Manning Provincial Park, 155
Manzanita Spring, *126*
Mariposa Battalion, 245
Mariposa Grove, 246
Mariscal, 19
Marymere Falls, *166*
Maze, 41
McKittrick Canyon, 117, *123, 124*
Merced Grove, 246
Merced River, 245, 246
Mesa Arches, *46, 48*
Mesa Verde National Park, 41, 133, *134-*
    144
Midway Geyser Basin, *232*
Mills, Enos, 187
Minerva Spring, *229*
Mirror Lake, *253*
Mississippi River, 7
Moab Fault, 10
Moran Point, *90*

Morning Glory Pool, *234*
Moro Rock, *206-207, 209*
Mount Dana, *253*
Mount Gibbs, *256*
Mount Mazama, 63
Mount Olympus, 162
Mount Rainier National Park, 8, 145, 146, *147-154,* 155
Mount Rushmore National Memorial, 279, *280-286*
Mount Shasta, 127, 155
Mount St. Helens, 63, 127, 146, 155
Mount Tehama, 127
Mount Whitney, 205
Muir, John, 146, 245, 246
National Elk Refuge, 96
National Park Service, 7, 8, 10, 20, 83, 96, 107, 214, 245, 246, 257
Nature Loop Trail, *125*
Navajo, 10, 83, 133
Navajo/Queens Garden Trail, *35, 38, 39*
Navajo Sandstone, 51
Needles, 41, *42, 43, 44, 46, 49*
Never Summer Ranch, *197, 201*
Newspaper Rock, *50,* 173
North Cascades National Park, 63, 127, 145, 146, 155, *156-160,* 179
North Rim, 31, *85, 86*
North Window, *15*
Nymph Lake, *191*
Oak Tree House, *143*
Old Faithful, 213, 214, *237*
Old Fall River Road, *200*
Olmsted Point, *256*
Olympic National Park, 161, 162, *163-172*
Olympic Peninsula, 8, 161, 179
Oregon Dunes National Recreation Area, *276-277*
Organic Act, 8
Ouzel Falls, *192*
Oxbow Bend Turnout, *102*
Pacific Plate, 127
Pacific Ring of Fire, 127, 146
Painted Desert, 83, 84, 173
Painted Desert Inn, 173
Paradise Park, 145
Paunsaugunt Plateau, 31
Petrified Forest National Park, 173, *174-178*
Phantom Ship, *66, 67*
Pike, Lt. Zebulon, 187
Pine Tree Arch, *11, 16*
Pink Cliffs, 31
Porcelain Basin, *224-226*
Pothole Point Trail, *45*
Powell, John Wesley, 84, 187
    Exploration of the Colorado River of the West and Its Tributaries, 84
Powell Plateau, *88*
Pratt, Wallace, 117
Puerco Indian Ruin, 173
Rainbow Point, *38*
Redwood Creek, 179
Redwood National Park, 179, *180-186*
Reflection Lake, *151, 154*
Revolutionary War, 8
Rialto Beach, *167*
Rio Grande, 19, 20, *25, 26, 27, 30*
River Falls, *209*
River of the Holy Kings, 205
Roadside Ruin Trail, *50*
Roaring Mountain, *226*
Robinson, Doane, 279
Rockefeller, 96
Rocky Mountain National Park, 72, 96, 107, 162, 187, *188-204*
Roosevelt, President Franklin Delanore, 161, 283
Roosevelt, President Theodore, 8, 84, 127,

161, 162, *186,* 279, *280-281*
Ross Lake Recreation Area, 155, *156-157*
Ruby Beach, *163, 164*
Salt Creek, 10
San Andreas Fault, 127
Sand Dune Arch, *17*
San Francisco Peaks, 84
Santa Fe Railroad, 173
Santa Helena Canyon, 19, *25, 30*
Scenic Drive, 51, *58*
Sequoia/Kings Canyon National Parks, 8, 205, *206-212*
Shell Canada, 72
Sherburne Lake, *79, 82*
Sierra Club, 146, 246
Sierra Madre, 19
Skyline Arch, 9, *15*
Smokey the Bear, 213
Snake Creek, 107
Snake Range, 107
Snake River, 96, *98*
Sonoran Desert, 107
Sotol Vista, *28*
South Rim, *87, 90, 91, 94*
Spruce Tree House, *139-141*
Square Tower House, *136-137, 142*
Steamboat Geyser, *236*
Stella Lake, 107
Stevens, Hazard, 146
St. Mary Lake, *76, 81*
Stone Age, 133
String Lake, *103*
Sundrift Gorge, *78*
Sun Point, *81*
Sun Temple, 133
Swiftcurrent Lake, *77*
Swiss Alps, 95
Tall Trees Grove, 179
Teton Fault, 95, 96
Thoreau, Henry David, 213, 265
Tower Falls, *219*
Trail View Point, *90*
Triple-Divide Peak, 71
Trump, Philemon Beecher Van, 146
Tuff Canyon, *23*
Tunnel View, *252, 254, 255*
Tuolumne, 246
Turnbow Cabin, 10
Turret Arch, *16, 17*
United Nations Educational, Scientific & Cultural Organization, 71
Upheaval Dome, 41
Vernal Falls, *250, 251*
Vidae Falls, *69*
Wahkeena Falls, *160*
Walden Pond, 265
War in the Pacific Park, 8
Washington, George, 279, *280-281*
Waterpocket Fold, 51
Waterton/Glacier International Peace Park, 8, 20, 71, 72, *73-82,* 84, 213
West Thumb Geyser Basin, *236, 238*
Wheeler Peak, 107, *109, 112, 113*
White, Jim, 59
White Sands National Monument, *270-271, 273*
Wild Goose Island, *81*
Williams Ranch, *120*
Willow Flats, 96
The Windows, *16*
Window Trail, *21, 22*
Wizard Island, 63, *68*
Wolfe, John, 10
Wolverton, James, 205
Yellowstone National Park, 7, 8, 20, 72, 84, 95, 96, 162, 213, 214, *215-244,* 265
Yellowstone River, 214, *220-221, 229*
Yaki Point, *92-93*
Yosemite National Park, 7, 8, 20, 117, 205,

214, 245, 246, *247-256,* 265
Yosemite Valley, 245, 246, *249, 250, 252, 254*
Zabriskie Point, *269*
Zion Canyon, 257, *262*
Zion/Mt. Carmel Highway, *259, 260, 264*
Zion National Park, 257, *258-264*